VITAL STATISTICS FOR YOUR VETERINARY PRACTICE

Financial and Productivity Pulsepoints

A COMPREHENSIVE SURVEY AND ANALYSIS OF PERFORMANCE BENCHMARKS

AAHA PRESS

Financial and Productivity Pulsepoints

12575 West Bayaud Avenue
Lakewood, Colorado 80228
800/252-2242 or 303/986-2800
Printed in the USA

ISBN 0-941451-68-2

This book was designed and typeset in Giovanni and Antique Olive by Stephen Adams, Aspen.

10 9 8 7 6 5 4 3 2 1

AAHA Management Services

We know it takes more than good medicine to make a practice successful.

Practice management consulting
Financial and productivity analysis
Demographic reports
Survey and analysis of staff needs
Practice management continuing education
Veterinary-specific management books
Staff training resources
Client education materials
Retirement program
Workers' compensation insurance
Business owner's insurance
Disability insurance
Credit cards for pet health care
Practice managers' job bank

Contents

Acknowledgments v
About the Author vi
Introduction vii
Key Findings x
Research Methodology xii
Cost-of-Living Index xiii
Regions xiv

Staff 1
- Number of Full-time Equivalent Veterinarians 2
- Number of Full-time Equivalent Nonveterinarian Staff 4
- Number of Nonveterinarian Staff per Veterinarian 6

Income 9
- Gross Income 1996 10
- Gross Income 1997 11
- Gross Income Growth Rate from 1996 to 1997 12
- Laboratory Income as a Percentage of Gross Income 14
- Radiology Income as a Percentage of Gross Income 16
- Dentistry Income as a Percentage of Gross Income 18
- Ancillary Services Income as a Percentage of Gross Income 20

Productivity 23
- Income per Veterinarian 24
- Number of Transactions per Veterinarian 28
- Average Transaction Charge (ATC) 30

Expenses 33
- Drugs and Medical Supplies Expense as a Percentage of Gross Income 34
- Laboratory Expense as a Percentage of Gross Income 36
- Ancillary Services Expense as a Percentage of Gross Income 38
- Associate Veterinarians Salary Expense as a Percentage of Gross Income 40
- Nonveterinarian Staff Salary Expense as a Percentage of Gross Income 42
- Employee Benefits Program Expense as a Percentage of Gross Income 44
- Rent/Lease of Facility Expense as a Percentage of Gross Income 46
- Total Expenses as a Percentage of Gross Income 48
- Net Income before Owner Compensation as a Percentage of Gross Income 50
- Total Salaries/Draw Paid to Owners as a Percentage of Gross Income 52

Assets and Liabilities 55
Cash and Cash Equivalents 56
Accounts Receivable 58
Accounts Receivable as a Percentage of Gross Income 59
Inventory 62
Current Assets 64
Total Assets 66
Current Liabilities 68
Total Liabilities 70
Total Equity 72
Current Ratio 74
Quick Ratio 76
Equity to Asset Ratio 78

Feline Practice Analysis 80

Canadian Practice Analysis 84

Emergency and Critical Care Practice Analysis 88

Appendix 95
U.S. Total (Mixed and Small) 96
Mixed Practices 97
Small Animal Practices 98

New England 99
Mid-Atlantic 100
South 101
Great Lakes 102
Plains 103
Northern Mountains 104
West 105
Pacific Northwest 106
Southwest 107
South Atlantic 108
Northern California 109
Southern California 110

One Veterinarian 111
1.1–3 Veterinarians 112
3.1–5 Veterinarians 113
5+ Veterinarians 114

<$250,000 Gross Income 115
$250,000–$500,000 Gross Income 116
$750,000–$1,000,000 Gross Income 117
$1,000,000+ Gross Income 118

Low Cost-of-Living States 119
Average Cost-of-Living States 120
High Cost-of-Living States 121

Acknowledgments

The achievement of this survey and publication of this reference required the commitment and dedication of many individuals.

Special thanks to Dr. Robert E. Froehlich, former director of AAHA's hospital and management group. His vision and commitment to quality on this project is greatly appreciated. Also a special thanks to the team members who designed the survey instrument: Ms. Leslie Mamalis, Ms. Terri Krantz, Ms. Crystal Wilcox, and Mr. Steve Schulberg.

This reference would not be possible without the significant contribution of one of AAHA's management consultants, Ms. Erin Bohlender. Her expertise, detailed explanations, positive attitude, and relentless will to keep the project afloat cannot be underestimated.

Thank you to the members of the Council of 100 and the AAHA Press Editorial Advisory Board. Your feedback and review of the project is greatly appreciated.

A special thank you to Mr. Ian McClure, Mr. Richard Lee, and Mr. Jared Rosckes of the DVM Group for their role in the analysis of the data. We support their growing operation and hope that veterinarians take advantage of their specialized financial and administrative services by contacting them at: The DVM Group, 14160 Dallas Parkway, Suite 880, Dallas, TX 75240. Phone 888/870/4135.

Finally, and most importantly, AAHA would like to acknowledge the veterinarians who gave their time and effort to complete and return the survey. This reference would still be only an idea without their dedication to the profession.

Dana McCullah
AAHA Press General Manager and Project Leader

About the Author

Ms. Erin Bohlender, MS, CPA has been with the American Animal Hospital Association for over eight years. Currently, Erin is a management consultant for AAHA and works through financial, staff, and other management issues with hundreds of practice owners and managers each year. She has worked with third party vendors such as CareCredit and the members' insurance programs. Erin also managed AAHA's Practice Edge Management Reports project for two years, where she helped members turn their financial and productivity information into higher profits and well-managed practices. Ms. Bohlender is a regular reviewer of AAHA Press management titles and contributes to *TRENDS magazine.* Erin is a Certified Public Accountant with an undergraduate degree in Business Management and a Master's degree in Accounting.

Introduction

Many managers and practice owners need some way to compare their performance to that of similar practices. AAHA conducted this survey to give the veterinary profession the information they need to do just that. And rather than just giving you the data, we explain what it means and how to use it in your practice.

AAHA strives to help small animal veterinary health care teams provide the very best service they can to their clients and patients. This book supports that mission by helping you understand how you can maximize productivity and profitability. Higher profits mean you can do two very important things:

1. Reinvest in:

- Remodeling, renovating, or building so you can maintain warm and inviting facilities for your clients and comfortable environments for your patients
- New equipment to provide high-quality care for patients and peace of mind for clients
- Recruiting and maintaining the kind of staff who make your practice something to be proud of

2. Invest in yourself! Take a vacation once in a while, spend time with your friends and family, and live a comfortable life. If you do so, you will be ready to give your clients and your patients 100% of your energy every day.

Why Is This Information Important?

This book is a management tool designed to help you identify your practice's strengths and weaknesses so you can maximize productivity, generate more revenue, and control expenses. Many practice owners and managers judge how well their practices are doing by whether or not January 1999 was better than January 1998 or by whether or not any cash is in the bank at month's end. There is no doubt about it: Having money to pay yourself is certainly important, as is comparing current performance to past performance.

But you need to compare yourself to a "norm" in order to understand how you compare to other practices. How do you know if you are producing as much as you should be? If you are producing as much as the high-end performers? If your average transaction charge (ATC) is high enough? If you are spending too much on drugs and supplies? If your accounts receivable are too high? You do not know this information until you have some frame of reference. That's where this book comes in.

Using Percentages to Compare Your Practice to Others

A common question we hear is: "How can you possibly compare my three-doctor, $900,000 practice to an average that includes everything from one-doctor, $150,000 practices to multi-million dollar practices?" It may seem impossible, but by using a method called *common-size analysis,* we can equate practices of varying sizes. When we use this method, we measure your income and expense dollar amounts as a *percentage of the practice's gross income.*

The dollar amount of any given income or expense category varies widely from practice to practice but the percentage of gross income is approximately the same for each practice.

> *Example: Suppose a practice that grosses $300,000 a year spends $42,000 annually on drugs and supplies whereas an $800,000-a-year practice spends $112,000 annually on drugs and supplies. The dollar amounts of $42,000 and $112,000 are very different, but each practice is spending 14% of gross income on drugs and supplies. By calculating averages in this way, we can give you meaningful statistics that you can use to compare your performance to the norm.*

Common-size analysis is a valid and well-recognized tool that financial analysts use to compare different-sized businesses in the same industry.

What Is a Percentile?

This book reports four values for each item reported: 25th percentile, median, average, and 75th percentile. These values give you more than just an "average" to which you can compare your practice's performance.

The *25th percentile* is the number at which 25% of the responses were below the reported value and 75% of the responses were above it.

The *median* (*50th percentile*) is the center point. In other words, 50% of the responses were above that number and 50% were below it.

> *Example: In the following list of staff salary expense percentages, the median is 21% because half of the values in the list are below 21% and half are above 21%:*
>
> *18%, 18%, 18%, 20%, 21%, 23%, 23.5%, 25.5%, 27%*

Note that the median is not the same as the *average,* or *mean,* which is 21.6%. A median may be a truer picture of the "average" practice than the average because the median is not skewed by extremely high or extremely low values. It is still an imperfect measure, however.

The *75th percentile* is the number at which 75% of the responses were below the number reported and 25% of the responses were above it.

Note: All Graphs display the median values.

How to Use Financial and Productivity Pulsepoints to Diagnose Your Practice

While evaluating the benchmark information, it is important that you view it from several angles. For example, you can reference your own practice's numbers against those of your region, the cost-of-living index (COL), the number of full-time equivalent veterinarians, and the gross income. In addition, we separate mixed practices, feline practices, and emergency/critical care practices from small animal practices. Practices in Canada are segmented separately as well.

For example, let's say your practice is a small animal practice and is in the West region with 2 veterinarians with a gross income of $600,000. You would then want to reference the small animal practice and West regional figures, as well as the sections for the practices with 1.1 to 3 veterinarians and the section for practices with gross income between $500,000 and $750,000 for each data point.

If you look at the data from several angles, you can take advantage of the information more efficiently and make educated adjustments in your operations.

The COL index shows what a certain "bundle" of goods would cost from one region to the next. Included in this "bundle" of goods are such items as food, clothing, housing, transportation, and drug and medical supply expenses.

The index is expressed with a basis of 100 being the norm. Therefore, when you contrast two states, one with an index of 102.84 (Pennsylvania) and one with an index of 97.59 (Kansas), you will notice the difference. A "bundle" of goods that costs $102.84 in Pennsylvania costs approximately $97.59 in Kansas. Therefore, it costs more to live in Pennsylvania than it does to live in Kansas.

The COL index is helpful when you are comparing different practices' ATCs, gross income, and salary expense percentages. You can reference all these data points to those in the COL index in order to equate living standards. See page xiii for more information on the COL index.

Where to Go From Here

Once you have read *Financial and Productivity Pulsepoints*, and learned what they are all about, what can you do with the information? You can make your practice more profitable and more efficient! Once you have identified strengths and weaknesses in your practice, the next step is to organize an action plan.

The best way to improve your practice's performance is to decide on one or two areas where you feel you need to improve the most. Then, formulate an action plan with small steps, assigning a deadline to each step and a person to complete each step. Remember: If you try to change everything at once, you and your staff will be easily overwhelmed and you will find it simpler to do nothing at all.

Sometimes, an objective third party is better able to help you create and monitor an action plan. Call AAHA's Management Services at 800/252-2242 if you need help:

- Interpreting this data compared to that for your own practice
- Formulating an action plan
- Finding management resources
- Periodically evaluating your progress toward your goals

You are not alone when it comes to managing your practice! AAHA is here to help you succeed.

Key Findings

Although you really need to dig into the information on the following pages to determine how well your practice is performing, these highlights give you an overview of some of the major points in this book.

Staff

- The typical U.S. practice has a median of 2.0 veterinarians, 6.0 full-time equivalent nonveterinarian staff, and 3.0 nonveterinarian staff for every veterinarian. Most practices have 3.0 or fewer veterinarians.
- Adding veterinarians does not require adding more nonveterinarian staff per veterinarian. In other words, the median number of nonveterinarian staff per veterinarian is 3.0 no matter how many veterinarians are in the practice.
- Feline practices have a median number of 1.0 veterinarian and 3.5 nonveterinarian staff per veterinarian.
- About 2 nonveterinarian staff are added for every $250,000 increment in gross income.

Productivity

- Practices with high gross incomes also have high incomes per veterinarian. Rather than increasing the gross income by hiring more veterinarians who produce at the same average rate, practices are increasing the gross income by producing more per veterinarian.
- The U.S. median number of transactions per veterinarian per year is 4,634. Emergency/critical care veterinarians generate a median of 2,044 transactions per veterinarian per year.
- Emergency/critical care practices partially compensate for their lower transaction numbers with a median ATC of $112.12, which is almost twice the U.S. median of $59.76.
- The regional medians for income per veterinarian range from $237,000 to $380,157 and the U.S. median is about $279,000. Practices in Canada have a median income per veterinarian of $181,380 in U.S. dollars.
- One-veterinarian practices produce a U.S. median gross income 1997 of $305,500 and can produce up to $500,000 by adding a part-time associate (a nonowner veterinarian working 1/3 time, or about 12 hours per week). Thereafter, every $250,000 jump in gross income requires the addition of another full-time veterinarian.
- There is a correlation between the ATC and the cost of living (COL). The high COL states tend to have higher ATCs.

Gross Income

- The U.S. median for gross income in 1996 is $576,299; $622,541 in 1997. The averages are $650,112 and $707,704, respectively.
- The U.S. median gross income growth rate from 1996 to 1997 is 7.5%, and the average is 8.8%. Mixed animal practices grew at a

slightly slower rate than small animal practices; feline practices grew at twice the U.S. median rate.

- The U.S. median for laboratory income as a percentage of gross income is 11.9%. Feline practices have the highest value of 17.5% and practices in Canada have the lowest value of 7.7%.
- The median markup on laboratory services is 350%, but this figure varies widely depending on practice size and location. As a practice grows, the laboratory expense percentages increase and the markup on laboratory services decreases.
- Most U.S. practices derive a median of 2.9% of their gross income from radiology services. Practices in California have a median radiology income in the 4.5% range.
- The percentage of gross income from ancillary services (boarding, grooming, food, and over-the-counter items) varies quite a bit, with a U.S. median of 13.3%. Practice size does not seem to be a factor in the amount of income earned from ancillary services. The median markup on these services is 200%.
- Dentistry income is only 1% to 2% of most practices' gross income.

Expenses

- The U.S. median drug and medical supply expense as a percentage of gross income is 15.6%, with feline practices having a low of only 10.8% and mixed practices having a high of 18.1%. Emergency/critical care practices have median drug and medical supply expense of 11.7%.
- Ancillary services expense percentages vary widely across all regions and practice sizes. Most U.S. practices have a median ancillary services expense percentage of between 4% and 5%. The exception is practices in Canada, which spend over 7% of their gross income on ancillary services.
- The salary expense of nonveterinarian staff as a percentage of gross income is fairly uniform across all practice types and regions, with the U.S. median being 20% of a practice's gross income. The largest practices do spend about 2 percentage points more on nonveterinarian staff salaries than the smallest practices.
- The U.S. median for employee benefits program expense as a percentage of gross income is 2%. Practices with <$250,000 in gross income spend 1.2% of their gross income on employee benefits; practices with $1,000,000+ in gross income spend 2.3%.
- The U.S. median for rent/lease of facility expense as a percentage of gross income is 5.7%. Rent/lease of facility expense decreases as a practice's gross income increases.
- Total expenses as a percentage of gross income are fairly uniform across all practice types and regions with a U.S. median of 75.1%. (This total expense number does not include owner compensation.) Emergency/critical care practices tend to have a higher total expense percentage of almost 81%. Their higher total expense percentage is due in part to the fact that they employ a relatively higher number of nonowner veterinarians.
- Most practice owners take a median of 17.7% of the practice's gross income in compensation. The exception is feline practices, whose owners typically take a salary of 11.7% of the practice's gross income. As practices grow, owners take less compensation as a percentage of gross income.

Assets and Liabilities

- The U.S. median cash balance is $16,549, but the numbers vary a fair amount depending on region and practice size. The U.S. median for cash as a percentage of gross income is 2.7%.
- Accounts receivable as a percentage of gross income increases as the practice size increases (from 1.1% in 1-veterinarian practices to 2.3% in 5+ veterinarian practices).
- The median for inventory is $20,000 for small animal practices and $25,264 for mixed practices. Inventory increases as practice size increases. One-veterinarian practices carry a median of $15,000 in inventory, while 5+ veterinarian practices carry a median of $58,201 in inventory.
- The U.S. median current ratio is 1.14:1 and the U.S. average is 2.42:1. At least 50% of the practices have $1.14 in current assets for every $1.00 in current debt.

Research Methodology

AAHA conducted a benchmark survey by randomly selecting a sample of veterinary practices (both members and non-members) from the AAHA database. Questionnaires were mailed to 10,000 practices within the United States and Canada in January 1998.

A total of 584 surveys were returned by early April, representing almost a 6% response rate. This response rate means there is a possibility of non-response bias in the findings if those who chose to participate differ in some systematic way from those who did not respond.

While there was no specific verification of the overall representativeness of those who did return questionnaires, the demographic distributions of responses show that the sample includes practices in every state and province with a wide range of practice sizes represented. Thus, while we cannot state with certainty that the results obtained represent the "typical" veterinary practice, the findings do provide a benchmark for comparison of your practice to a number of other similar practices.

The number of responses varies for each individual measure reported and is highlighted within each table for your reference.

Cost-of-Living Index

The Cost-of-Living (COL) index used in this publication has followed the ACCRA Cost-of-Living Index. Founded in 1961, the American Chamber of Commerce Researchers Association is a non-profit organization consisting of chambers of commerce, economic development organizations, and related organizations throughout the United States.

ACCRA bases its Cost-of-Living Index on consumer surveys of expenditures for consumer goods such as food, clothing, housing, transportation, and medical expenses. All items are priced in each geographic location at the same time and according to standardized specifications.

The areas included in the ACCRA Cost-of-Living Index are those where chambers of commerce or similar organizations have volunteered to participate. When states are not represented in ACCRA's indexes it is because the chambers of commerce in those states have opted not to collect and report data to ACCRA. The states that are therefore not in the COL tables in this publication are Hawaii, Maine, New Hampshire, New Jersey, and Rhode Island.

Based on ACCRA's research, AAHA has constructed the following low, average, and high COL groups for the purposes of this report:

Low	Average	High
Alabama	Colorado	Alaska
Arkansas	Florida	Arizona
Georgia	Illinois	California
Idaho	Iowa	Connecticut
Indiana	Maryland	Delaware
Kansas	Minnesota	Massachusetts
Kentucky	Montana	Michigan
Louisiana	New Mexico	Nevada
Mississippi	North Carolina	New York
Missouri	Pennsylvania	Oregon
Nebraska	South Dakota	Vermont
North Dakota	Utah	Washington, D.C.
Ohio	Washington	
Oklahoma	West Virginia	
South Carolina	Wisconsin	
Tennessee		
Texas		
Virginia		
Wyoming		

Regions

This publication reports information by geographic region. The following list shows the states that are included in each region.

New England	Mid Atlantic	South	South Atlantic
Connecticut	Delaware	Kentucky	Alabama
Maine	Maryland	North Carolina	Arkansas
Massachusetts	New Jersey	South Carolina	Florida
New Hampshire	New York	Tennessee	Georgia
Rhode Island	Pennsylvania	Virginia	Louisiana
Vermont	Puerto Rico	West Virginia	Mississippi
	Washington, D.C.		

Great Lakes	Plains	Northern Mountains	West
Illinois	Iowa	Idaho	Colorado
Indiana	Kansas	Montana	New Mexico
Michigan	Minnesota	Wyoming	Oklahoma
Ohio	Missouri		Texas
Wisconsin	Nebraska		
	North Dakota		
	South Dakota		

Pacific Northwest	Southwest
Alaska	Arizona
Hawaii	Nevada
Oregon	Utah
Washington	

Northern California

From the southern San Francisco bay area, including San Jose and areas north.

Southern California

All areas in California south of the Northern California area.

Canada

All practices that responded to the survey that are located in Canada.

Staff

NUMBER OF FULL-TIME EQUIVALENT VETERINARIANS

General Overview	25th Percentile	Median	Average	75th Percentile	Number of Responses
U.S. Total (Mixed and Small)	1.3	2.0	2.4	3.0	584
Mixed Practices	1.3	2.0	2.5	3.4	128
Small Animal Practices	1.3	2.0	2.4	3.0	467
Feline Practices	1.0	1.0	1.4	1.5	19
Emergency/Critical Care Practices	3.9	4.6	5.9	7.7	24
Canada Total	1.5	2.5	2.6	3.3	43
Segmented by Region					
New England	2.0	2.0	2.6	3.4	32
Mid-Atlantic	1.3	2.0	2.6	3.3	57
South	1.3	2.0	2.2	3.0	76
Great Lakes	1.5	2.3	2.6	3.3	117
Plains	1.3	2.0	2.3	3.3	48
Northern Mountains	1.0	2.1	1.9	2.5	6
West	1.2	2.0	2.1	2.5	63
Pacific Northwest	1.5	2.0	2.5	3.2	29
Southwest	1.3	2.6	2.6	3.8	28
South Atlantic	1.0	2.0	2.3	3.0	57
Northern California	1.2	1.8	2.4	3.0	29
Southern California	1.3	2.0	2.3	3.0	21
Segmented by Number of Veterinarians					
1 Veterinarian	1.0	1.0	1.0	1.0	117
1.1–3 Veterinarians	1.5	2.0	1.9	2.0	274
3.1–5 Veterinarians	3.0	3.5	3.6	4.0	162
5+ Veterinarians	5.0	5.5	6.2	6.3	34
Segmented by Gross Income					
< $250,000 Gross Income	1.0	1.0	1.1	1.0	44
$250,000–$500,000 Gross Income	1.0	1.3	1.5	2.0	155
$500,000–$750,000 Gross Income	2.0	2.0	2.2	2.5	169
$750,000–$1,000,000 Gross Income	2.3	3.0	2.9	3.5	105
$1,000,000+ Gross Income	3.5	4.0	4.4	5.0	103
Segmented by Cost-of-Living Indices					
Low Cost-of-Living States	1.0	2.0	2.2	3.0	181
Average Cost-of-Living States	1.5	2.0	2.6	3.2	217
High Cost-of-Living States	1.3	2.0	2.5	3.5	144

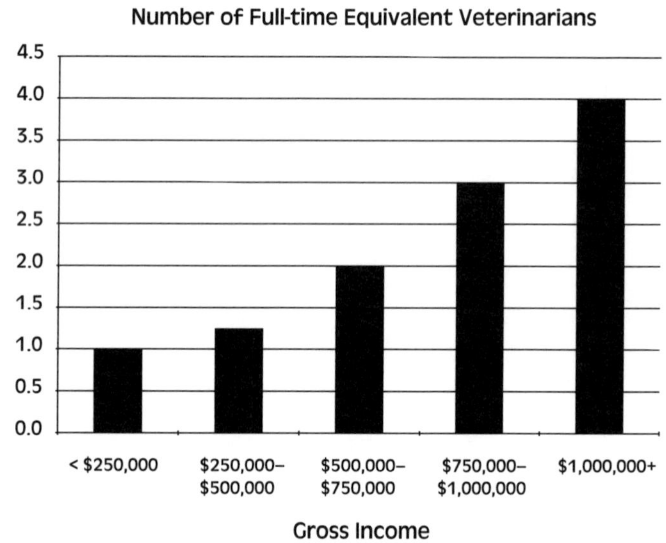

Number of Full-time Equivalent Veterinarians

Description

This is the number of full-time equivalent veterinarians who work in the practice, counting part-time veterinarians as fractions of a 40-hour work week (e.g., a veterinarian who works 30 hours per week is counted as 0.75 full-time equivalents). This number gives you a framework for interpreting the rest of the data.

For example, when you look at the U.S. median number of non-veterinarian staff per veterinarian and the U.S. median income per veterinarian, you know that those numbers are for the "typical" practice, which has a U.S. median of 2.0 full-time veterinarians per practice. Also, you know that the U.S. median inventory and accounts receivable are for a practice with a median of 2.0 veterinarians.

Significant Findings

The median practice in the United States is comprised of 2.0 veterinarians. The 75th percentile is 3.0 veterinarians, which indicates that most practices have 3 or fewer veterinarians.

If you refer to the part of the table segmented by gross income, you will see that the median number of veterinarians for the practices making <$250,000 is 1.0. The median number of veterinarians for the practices grossing $250,000–$500,000 is 1.3.

This data suggests that 1-veterinarian practices can produce up to $500,000 by adding a part-time associate veterinarian. Thereafter, every $250,000 jump in gross income requires the addition of another veterinarian. However, if you look at the analysis by income per veterinarian (see page 24), you see that it is not just adding veterinarians that makes a practice grow. Rather, the higher the practice's gross income, the more income per veterinarian the practice produces. Therefore, it is not just adding veterinarians that makes a practice grow; it is adding the right veterinarians, those who are high producers.

NUMBER OF FULL-TIME EQUIVALENT NONVETERINARIAN STAFF

General Overview	25th Percentile	Median	Average	75th Percentile	Number of Responses
U.S. Total (Mixed and Small)	4.0	6.0	7.6	9.8	580
Mixed Practices	3.5	5.5	6.7	8.5	125
Small Animal Practices	4.0	6.0	7.8	10.0	466
Feline Practices	2.4	4.0	4.7	5.3	19
Emergency/Critical Care Practices	6.3	11.8	16.7	21.3	28
Canada Total	3.0	5.3	5.9	8.0	43
Segmented by Region					
New England	4.0	6.0	7.5	10.0	31
Mid-Atlantic	5.0	7.0	8.8	11.0	58
South	4.5	6.5	7.2	8.8	76
Great Lakes	4.0	6.0	7.4	9.4	116
Plains	3.8	5.0	6.5	8.0	48
Northern Mountains	3.5	6.3	6.3	7.5	6
West	3.5	5.5	7.1	8.0	62
Pacific Northwest	5.0	7.0	7.3	9.8	29
Southwest	4.0	7.0	8.8	11.8	28
South Atlantic	4.3	7.0	8.7	11.0	56
Northern California	4.0	6.0	7.3	9.0	28
Southern California	4.0	6.0	8.0	10.0	21
Segmented by Number of Veterinarians					
1 Veterinarian	2.0	3.0	3.4	4.0	114
1.1–3 Veterinarians	4.5	6.0	6.3	7.5	273
3.1–5 Veterinarians	7.0	10.0	10.6	12.5	161
5+ Veterinarians	14.0	19.5	19.9	25.0	33
Segmented by Gross Income					
< $250,000 Gross Income	1.5	2.0	2.5	3.0	44
$250,000–$500,000 Gross Income	3.0	4.0	4.3	5.0	156
$500,000–$750,000 Gross Income	5.0	6.0	6.5	7.5	168
$750,000–$1,000,000 Gross Income	7.0	8.3	9.0	10.5	105
$1,000,000+ Gross Income	12.0	15.0	15.8	20.0	101
Segmented by Cost-of-Living Indices					
Low Cost-of-Living States	4.0	6.0	7.2	9.3	180
Average Cost-of-Living States	4.0	6.5	7.8	9.7	216
High Cost-of-Living States	4.0	6.0	8.1	10.5	143

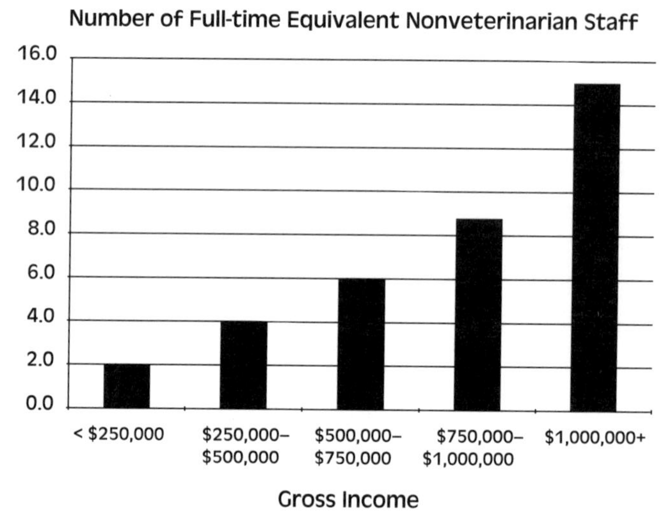

Number of Full-time Equivalent Nonveterinarian Staff

Description

This is the number of nonveterinarian staff who work in the practice, counting part-time people as fractions of a 40-hour workweek (e.g., a half-time receptionist is counted as 0.5 full-time equivalents).

You can also use this number, in conjunction with the number of nonveterinarian staff per veterinarian (see page 6) and the nonveterinarian staff salary expense percentage (see page 42), to evaluate if you are overstaffed or understaffed. You may have chosen to hire a larger-than-average nonveterinarian staff to provide a higher level of client service, which your practice's nonveterinarian staff salary expense will probably reflect. In other words, you should use your practice's gross income and desired level of customer service to determine your staff size. A small staff does not necessarily mean that you are running efficiently, just as a large staff does not equate to overstaffing.

Note that a large or small number of nonveterinarian staff in terms of absolute numbers is not significant when determining how many staff you "should" have. Instead, review the data in the next section: number of nonveterinarian staff per veterinarian (see page 6).

Significant Findings

The median practice in the United States employs 6.0 full-time equivalent nonveterinarian staff.

The data as segmented by gross income shows a pattern of a median of about 2 staff added for every $250,000 increment in gross income, except in the $1,000,000+ practices. In those practices, the median number of staff is 15.0, compared to the $750,000–$1,000,000 practices, which have a median staff of 8.3.

But also consider that the median gross income in 1997 for practices in the $750,000–$1,000,000 range is $849,699, and the median gross income for practices in the $1,000,000+ range is $1,258,509 (see page 11). This incremental jump in gross income is $408,810, compared to the $250,000 increment we mentioned before.

NUMBER OF NONVETERINARIAN STAFF PER VETERINARIAN

General Overview	25th Percentile	Median	Average	75th Percentile	Number of Responses
U.S. Total (Mixed and Small)	2.3	3.0	3.2	4.0	578
Mixed Practices	1.8	2.5	2.7	3.4	125
Small Animal Practices	2.5	3.1	3.3	4.0	464
Feline Practices	2.5	3.5	3.4	4.5	19
Emergency/Critical Care Practices	2.3	3.3	3.3	3.9	22
Canada Total	1.7	2.0	2.3	2.6	43
Segmented by Region					
New England	2.2	2.8	3.0	3.1	31
Mid-Atlantic	2.4	3.0	3.4	4.1	57
South	2.5	3.1	3.3	4.0	76
Great Lakes	2.0	2.7	2.9	3.6	115
Plains	1.8	2.7	2.8	3.3	48
Northern Mountains	2.1	3.1	3.3	3.8	6
West	2.5	3.5	3.3	4.0	62
Pacific Northwest	2.0	2.7	2.9	3.5	29
Southwest	2.5	3.5	3.3	4.0	28
South Atlantic	2.9	3.3	3.7	4.5	56
Northern California	2.5	2.9	2.9	3.3	28
Southern California	2.9	3.3	3.5	4.0	21
Segmented by Number of Veterinarians					
1 Veterinarian	2.0	3.0	3.4	4.0	114
1.1–3 Veterinarians	2.5	3.0	3.3	4.0	273
3.1–5 Veterinarians	2.0	2.9	3.0	3.8	161
5+ Veterinarians	2.6	2.9	3.2	3.7	33
Segmented by Gross Income					
< $250,000 Gross Income	1.5	2.0	2.2	3.0	44
$250,000–$500,000 Gross Income	2.0	3.0	3.0	3.8	154
$500,000–$750,000 Gross Income	2.0	2.8	3.0	3.5	168
$750,000–$1,000,000 Gross Income	2.1	3.0	3.1	4.0	105
$1,000,000+ Gross Income	2.8	3.4	3.6	4.1	101
Segmented by Cost-of-Living Indices					
Low Cost-of-Living States	2.3	3.0	3.3	4.0	180
Average Cost-of-Living States	2.2	3.0	3.1	3.8	214
High Cost-of-Living States	2.4	3.0	3.2	4.0	143

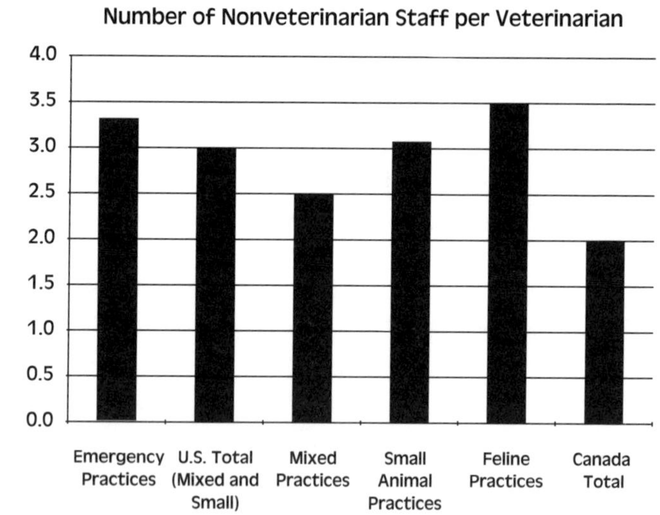

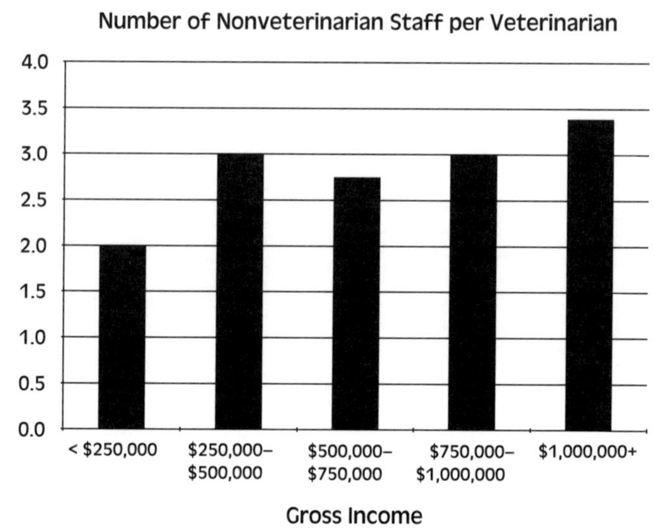

Number of Nonveterinarian Staff per Veterinarian

Definition

This represents the number of staff required to support one veterinarian. You should use this number in conjunction with your nonveterinarian staff salary expense to help you determine whether or not you are understaffed or overstaffed. Of course, you may have a higher or lower number of nonveterinarian staff per veterinarian, depending on how you use your staff and the level of client service you provide.

Significant Findings

The U.S. median ratio of nonveterinarian staff to veterinarians is 3.0:1. The median number of nonveterinarian staff per veterinarian varies from a high in feline practices (3.5:1) to a low in Canadian practices (2.0:1).

The number of nonveterinarian staff per veterinarian in mixed practices is lower than in small animal practices, with a ratio of 2.5:1 versus a ratio of 3.1:1, respectively. This is typically because the veterinarians in mixed practices see relatively fewer patients in the practice. Therefore, they need fewer staff to support the practice.

In the past, it was thought that 1-veterinarian practices typically required more nonveterinarian staff per veterinarian than other practices. However, the data does not bear this out. The U.S. median number of staff per veterinarian for 1-veterinarian practices is 3.0 and the average is 3.4. These numbers do not differ significantly from those of other practices as highlighted in the segmentation by number of veterinarians.

It is interesting to note how both the U.S. median and average number of staff per veterinarian vary according to gross income. Practices with a gross income of <$250,000 have a median of only 2.0 staff per veterinarian. On the other hand, practices with a gross income of $1,000,000+ report a median of 3.4. The smaller practices most likely need fewer staff because they are fledgling practices with a low volume of transactions. (This is borne out in the number of transactions per veterinarian as segmented by gross income as seen on page 28.)

However, the practices in the $1,000,000+ range do not differ significantly in number of transactions per veterinarian from their counterparts in the $750,000–$1,000,000 range (see page 28). Perhaps the largest practices use more middle management in order to manage the larger number of people who work in these practices, which then adds to overhead in the form of nonveterinarian staff salary expenses (see page 42).

Income

It is important to evaluate the structure of your revenue stream and how it compares to that of other practices. If you see that you are putting 20% of your resources (time, money, and personnel) into an income category that makes up 1% of gross income, it is time to reevaluate.

Or you may see that, in your region, dentistry income is an average of 3% of gross income while you consistently produce only 1%. Should you offer more of these services in order to compete with other practices? Gross income analysis certainly raises this type of question.

Although we recommend you segment your gross income into many categories, we have selected four key income categories for you to compare to those of your own practice: laboratory, radiology, dentistry, and ancillary services. If your percentages are lower than the medians, you need to consider whether or not you offer enough of these services to each client and whether your fees are where they should be. For fee comparisons, refer to *The Veterinary Fee Reference*, published by AAHA Press.

It is difficult to derive useful information from gross income numbers alone because you must also take into consideration the productivity and profit levels of the practice. It is important to review income per veterinarian along with other productivity measures such as transactions per veterinarian, average transaction charge (ATC), and total expenses as a percentage of gross income.

You also need to analyze how fast your gross income grows by comparing it to your region's rate of growth or perhaps to the growth rate in your state's COL index. Gross income should increase over time, as long as that goal is consistent with your long-term plans. Even if you have exactly the same number of transactions per veterinarian and offer the same services from year to year, your gross income should increase at least by the rate of inflation. If your practice's gross income does not increase by at least this much, you may have to consider raising your fees.

General Overview	25th Percentile	Median	Average	75th Percentile	Number of Responses
U.S. Total (Mixed and Small)	$381,580	$576,299	$650,112	$805,591	551
Mixed Practices	$372,202	$551,626	$620,820	$805,591	114
Small Animal Practices	$378,400	$577,529	$648,627	$800,288	448
Feline Practices	$240,000	$317,434	$371,800	$377,800	17
Emergency/Critical Care Practices	$509,520	$808,849	$1,003,634	$1,585,625	27
Canada Total (in Canadian dollars)	$381,084	$612,807	$694,902	$938,794	40
Segmented by Region					
New England	$450,493	$552,916	$734,332	$980,000	31
Mid-Atlantic	$412,813	$638,500	$737,063	$933,188	54
South	$357,878	$515,320	$568,780	$748,000	74
Great Lakes	$396,100	$589,922	$642,194	$789,215	112
Plains	$334,088	$510,250	$539,228	$694,335	45
Northern Mountains	$381,270	$517,100	$572,477	$757,304	5
West	$342,826	$461,021	$527,538	$607,650	56
Pacific Northwest	$377,790	$572,339	$579,223	$790,334	28
Southwest	$400,297	$684,694	$783,229	$1,023,895	26
South Atlantic	$345,397	$550,000	$644,267	$894,658	55
Northern California	$450,163	$597,763	$785,343	$878,234	28
Southern California	$469,000	$715,000	$841,417	$1,092,426	19
Segmented by Number of Veterinarians					
1 Veterinarian	$207,978	$302,539	$308,986	$385,000	103
1.1–3 Veterinarians	$388,539	$517,586	$532,157	$639,135	264
3.1–5 Veterinarians	$688,396	$862,080	$900,942	$1,040,000	153
5+ Veterinarians	$1,282,797	$1,585,874	$1,618,160	$1,840,887	32
Segmented by Gross Income					
< $250,000 Gross Income	$156,067	$177,560	$178,747	$200,462	37
$250,000–$500,000 Gross Income	$303,600	$356,939	$351,977	$394,600	154
$500,000–$750,000 Gross Income	$517,100	$576,281	$571,970	$627,127	165
$750,000–$1,000,000 Gross Income	$713,917	$790,669	$791,073	$860,836	99
$1,000,000+ Gross Income	$1,017,643	$1,153,812	$1,298,980	$1,464,417	96
Segmented by Cost-of-Living Indices					
Low Cost-of-Living States	$334,088	$506,000	$560,062	$687,767	173
Average Cost-of-Living States	$389,277	$588,708	$663,332	$814,513	207
High Cost-of-Living States	$425,683	$605,526	$719,906	$903,954	135

Gross Income 1996 and 1997

Definition

Gross income is the sum of income received from all medical services, ancillary services, interest, rent/lease of facility expenses, and other sources. Gross income does not include cash received from loans to the practice or other income that qualifies as an asset rather than income.

As mentioned on page 9, you must look at numbers other than gross income to gauge your performance. However, gross income does give you a frame of reference for interpreting the rest of the data.

Total Gross Income

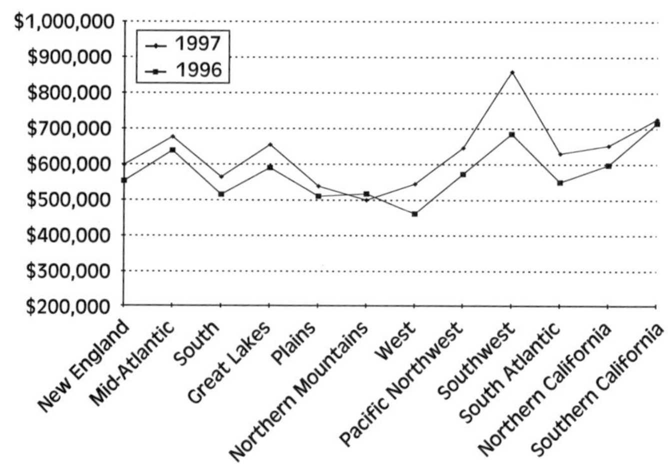

Significant Findings

The U.S. average is typically much higher than the median, which shows that many practices have high gross income numbers that skew the average upward. The U.S. median in 1996 is $576,299; in 1997 it is $622,541. The U.S. averages in 1996 and 1997 are $650,112 and $707,704, respectively.

Typically, the regions with the highest gross incomes are Southern California and the Southwest; the regions on the opposite side of the scale are the Plains, Northern Mountains, and the West.

As expected, gross income increases as the COL index increases.

1997 Gross Income

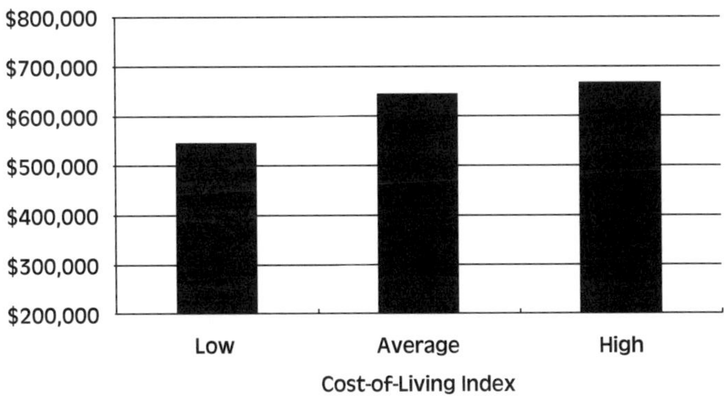

GROSS INCOME 1997

General Overview	25th Percentile	Median	Average	75th Percentile	Number of Responses
U.S. Total (Mixed and Small)	$412,000	$622,541	$707,704	$887,740	578
Mixed Practices	$412,217	$599,638	$687,961	$869,847	122
Small Animal Practices	$402,222	$618,879	$704,157	$887,740	467
Feline Practices	$245,227	$375,000	$409,454	$427,600	19
Emergency/Critical Care Practices	$566,578	$906,494	$1,192,938	$1,648,058	29
Canada Total (in Canadian dollars)	$389,730	$627,717	$705,388	$950,632	43
Segmented by Region					
New England	$483,769	$598,000	$797,451	$1,054,000	31
Mid-Atlantic	$474,993	$676,525	$807,967	$1,034,531	56
South	$367,751	$564,171	$619,454	$792,699	76
Great Lakes	$433,210	$654,790	$697,437	$860,097	116
Plains	$342,487	$538,626	$583,119	$808,599	48
Northern Mountains	$228,025	$499,497	$546,706	$771,427	6
West	$344,716	$545,113	$586,628	$684,827	62
Pacific Northwest	$416,000	$646,157	$685,131	$887,740	29
Southwest	$435,585	$860,000	$893,332	$1,104,260	28
South Atlantic	$375,000	$630,061	$711,935	$1,016,975	57
Northern California	$488,421	$652,332	$841,639	$898,480	28
Southern California	$475,196	$726,000	$813,823	$990,738	21
Segmented by Number of Veterinarians					
1 Veterinarian	$212,889	$305,500	$322,328	$384,158	109
1.1–3 Veterinarians	$432,029	$560,224	$584,737	$691,548	274
3.1–5 Veterinarians	$767,565	$925,453	$975,922	$1,109,000	162
5+ Veterinarians	$1,354,257	$1,161,423	$1,751,019	$1,971,000	34
Segmented by Gross Income					
< $250,000 Gross Income	$158,878	$199,050	$188,325	$212,979	44
$250,000–$500,000 Gross Income	$331,998	$383,000	$380,341	$432,029	157
$500,000–$750,000 Gross Income	$551,227	$619,819	$617,893	$675,584	169
$750,000–$1,000,000 Gross Income	$792,600	$849,699	$858,943	$917,678	105
$1,000,000+ Gross Income	$1,100,000	$1,258,509	$1,421,747	$1,639,037	103
Segmented by Cost-of-Living Indices					
Low Cost-of-Living States	$343,657	$546,058	$610,438	$774,451	180
Average Cost-of-Living States	$410,000	$646,000	$721,145	$899,424	217
High Cost-of-Living States	$472,948	$668,276	$784,045	$976,521	142

GROSS INCOME GROWTH RATE FROM 1996 TO 1997

General Overview	25th Percentile	Median	Average	75th Percentile	Number of Responses
U.S. Total (Mixed and Small)	3.5%	7.5%	8.8%	13.0%	556
Mixed Practices	2.0%	6.5%	7.8%	13.0%	117
Small Animal Practices	3.6%	8.0%	9.2%	13.2%	451
Feline Practices	10.8%	14.8%	19.4%	18.6%	18
Emergency/Critical Care Practices	3.9%	7.0%	9.1%	12.1%	27
Canada Total	1.6%	5.2%	5.4%	9.2%	40
Segmented by Region					
New England	4.2%	10.1%	8.6%	13.6%	31
Mid-Atlantic	3.8%	8.4%	10.6%	12.6%	54
South	3.0%	5.9%	7.7%	11.0%	74
Great Lakes	4.7%	8.2%	9.2%	13.2%	114
Plains	3.5%	7.0%	9.2%	12.0%	46
Northern Mountains	1.9%	13.6%	10.5%	15.8%	5
West	1.2%	6.3%	7.1%	10.6%	56
Pacific Northwest	3.0%	12.7%	10.3%	15.0%	28
Southwest	6.0%	8.1%	10.7%	11.1%	26
South Atlantic	3.6%	11.3%	10.8%	15.4%	55
Northern California	3.1%	6.3%	7.2%	10.9%	29
Southern California	–2.5%	2.9%	1.0%	7.7%	19
Segmented by Number of Veterinarians					
1 Veterinarian	2.4%	6.0%	8.1%	11.9%	107
1.1–3 Veterinarians	3.3%	8.1%	9.1%	13.5%	264
3.1–5 Veterinarians	3.5%	8.0%	8.7%	13.2%	153
5+ Veterinarians	4.2%	6.3%	8.2%	9.8%	32
Segmented by Gross Income					
< $250,000 Gross Income	2.4%	5.6%	11.0%	15.9%	39
$250,000–$500,000 Gross Income	2.3%	7.3%	8.0%	12.2%	154
$500,000–$750,000 Gross Income	2.7%	7.5%	8.1%	13.0%	165
$750,000–$1,000,000 Gross Income	4.5%	7.5%	8.4%	12.3%	99
$1,000,000+ Gross Income	4.2%	8.5%	9.7%	13.7%	96
Segmented by Cost-of-Living Indices					
Low Cost-of-Living States	3.0%	7.4%	8.6%	13.9%	174
Average Cost-of-Living States	4.5%	8.4%	9.3%	13.0%	209
High Cost-of-Living States	2.8%	6.7%	8.3%	12.3%	136

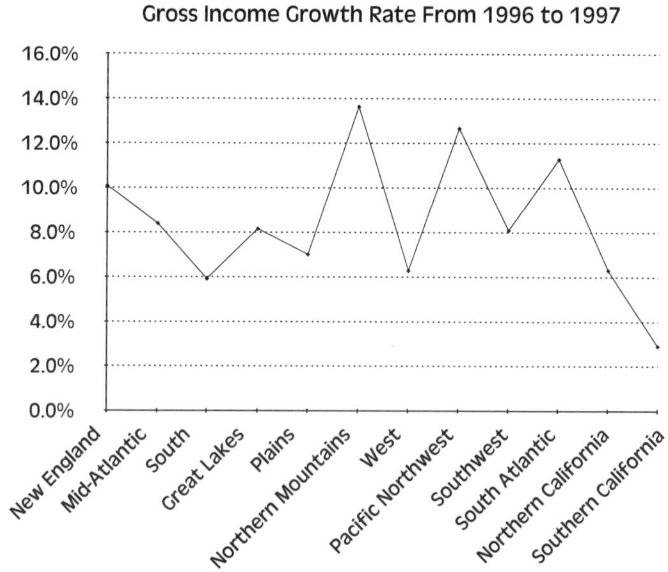

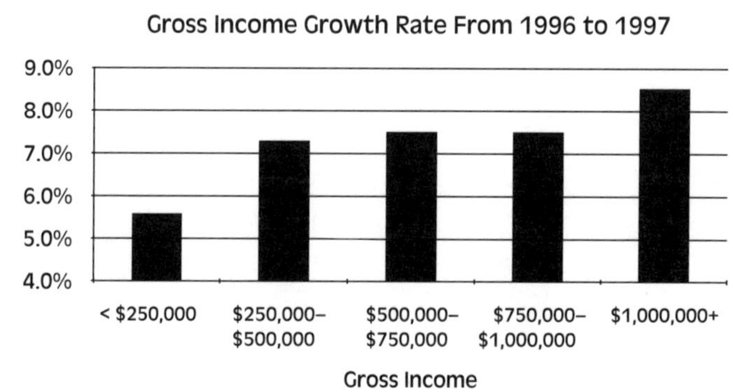

Gross Income Growth Rate From 1996 to 1997

Definition

The growth rate is calculated by dividing the difference between 1997 gross income and 1996 gross income by 1996 gross income.

$$\frac{\text{1997 gross income} - \text{1996 gross income}}{\text{1996 gross income}} = \text{\% growth rate}$$

This percentage shows you how fast practices are growing from one year to the next. Remember that growth in gross income does not necessarily mean growth in profit if you do not manage your growth properly. In other words, it is easy to spend more when you are making more without paying attention to whether or not the increase in spending results in a decrease in overall profit.

Growth in gross income may be due to increasing:

- Fees
- Client numbers
- The ATC
- The number of client visits per year
- The number or mix of services or products offered

When comparing your practice's growth rates to the data, it is important that you consider several factors. For example, younger practices will often experience significantly higher growth rates than established practices. Also, are you growing faster than the rate of inflation? If you are not outperforming inflation, your expenses will begin to increase in disproportion to your gross income. Your fees should increase each year by at least the rate of inflation (i.e., if the rate of inflation in your area is 3%, you should increase your fees by at least 3% to keep pace with inflation).

Growth in gross income in and of itself is not a measure of success. You also need to consider whether you are maintaining control over expenses. In other words, you do not want to grow your gross income only to net the same amount. Also, you must have the infrastructure in place to support growth. The right number of staff and veterinarians—along with appropriate internal policies, marketing strategies, and great customer service—should be in place before you attempt to grow your practice. Otherwise, the practice may very quickly grow past your ability to manage it. Lastly, you must have enough potential clients to support growth. Saying you want to grow and having the population in your area to realize that growth are two different things.

Significant Findings

The U.S. median growth rate was 7.5%, and the average was 8.8%. Mixed practices grew at a slightly lower rate than small animal practices, whereas feline practices grew at twice the U.S. median rate. The 75th percentile values were generally around 12% to 13%.

One region that falls short of this average is Southern California, with a median growth rate of 2.9%.

The South Atlantic and Pacific Northwest regions did particularly well, with median growth rates of 11.3% and 12.7%, respectively.

One-veterinarian practices demonstrated more variability in growth rates than did other practices, while 5+ veterinarian practices showed much less variability.

Practices in the $1,000,000+ gross income range had a median growth rate of 8.5%, while practices with <$250,000 in gross income had a median growth rate of 5.6%. However, the average for <$250,000 practices is 11%. These numbers indicate that a few practices in this gross income range are growing at a much faster rate than the others (most likely start-ups). Larger practices may have an easier time expanding because they have readier access to capital, which enables them to grow at a faster pace than smaller practices.

LABORATORY INCOME AS A PERCENTAGE OF GROSS INCOME

General Overview	25th Percentile	Median	Average	75th Percentile	Number of Responses
U.S. Total (Mixed and Small)	9.2%	11.9%	11.9%	14.5%	503
Mixed Practices	7.1%	9.6%	9.8%	11.8%	96
Small Animal Practices	9.9%	12.6%	12.5%	15.1%	418
Feline Practices	16.1%	17.5%	19.1%	24.6%	19
Emergency/Critical Care Practices	9.5%	11.5%	11.7%	12.6%	25
Canada Total	6.0%	7.7%	8.5%	10.5%	37
Segmented by Region					
New England	8.9%	11.4%	11.4%	13.7%	28
Mid-Atlantic	10.2%	12.7%	12.6%	14.9%	52
South	10.5%	12.0%	12.3%	14.3%	62
Great Lakes	10.4%	13.4%	13.2%	15.9%	107
Plains	10.0%	13.1%	12.7%	15.3%	42
Northern Mountains	4.0%	6.2%	5.9%	6.2%	5
West	8.8%	11.3%	11.4%	14.8%	56
Pacific Northwest	5.9%	8.9%	9.3%	12.0%	22
Southwest	7.8%	10.9%	10.4%	12.2%	22
South Atlantic	8.7%	11.6%	10.9%	13.4%	46
Northern California	8.1%	10.9%	10.6%	11.5%	23
Southern California	8.9%	12.8%	11.9%	14.2%	18
Segmented by Number of Veterinarians					
1 Veterinarian	7.5%	11.4%	11.0%	13.5%	94
1.1–3 Veterinarians	9.1%	11.9%	11.9%	14.5%	236
3.1–5 Veterinarians	9.1%	12.0%	12.0%	14.1%	144
5+ Veterinarians	9.3%	11.5%	11.7%	15.2%	29
Segmented by Gross Income					
< $250,000 Gross Income	8.1%	10.0%	10.3%	12.9%	35
$250,000–$500,000 Gross Income	8.1%	11.5%	11.2%	13.9%	137
$500,000–$750,000 Gross Income	10.0%	11.9%	12.2%	14.4%	149
$750,000–$1,000,000 Gross Income	8.8%	11.9%	12.0%	14.7%	92
$1,000,000+ Gross Income	9.2%	12.3%	12.0%	14.7%	87
Segmented by Cost-of-Living Indices					
Low Cost-of-Living States	8.9%	11.7%	11.4%	13.8%	155
Average Cost-of-Living States	9.3%	12.4%	12.0%	14.9%	188
High Cost-of-Living States	9.3%	11.5%	12.0%	14.1%	124

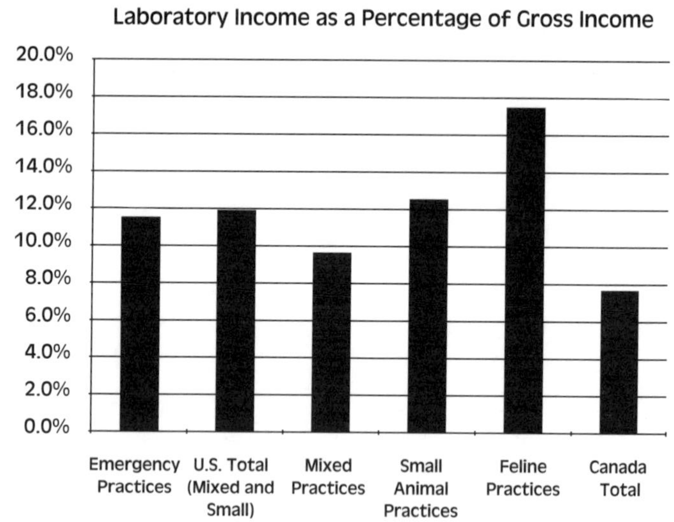

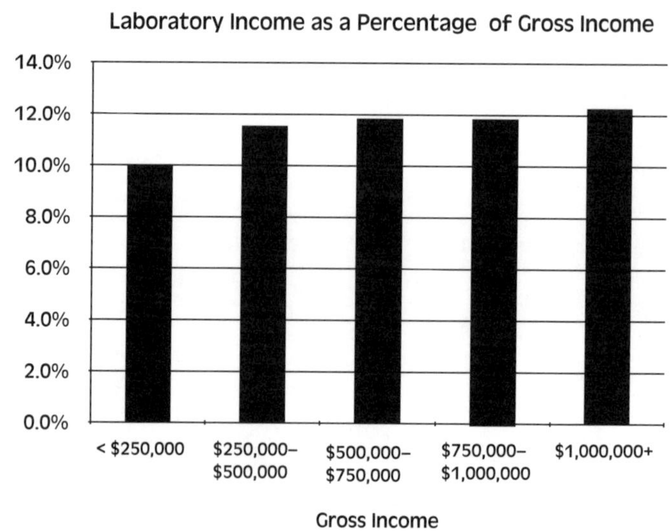

Laboratory Income as a Percentage of Gross Income

Definition

Laboratory income is a measure of two things: the volume of laboratory work you do and the fees you charge for those services. Increasing laboratory income is an easy way to increase your bottom line while providing good diagnostic services to your clients.

Examples of commonly missed opportunities in laboratory income are:

- Recommending pre-surgical laboratory screens
- Recommending getting baseline values for pets before they become geriatric and subsequent annual laboratory screens for geriatric patients
- Recommending annual screens for pets on heartworm preventatives
- Charging a blood/fluid drawing fee
- Adding the lease portion of the chemistry machine and technician time to your costs when determining your laboratory fees
- Having a second person ensure all laboratory services are recorded on the circle sheet daily

Review your laboratory income versus laboratory expenses (which, as we have defined it, do not include staff time or leasing/buying equipment) and compare those figures to the medians for your region. If you are not making the profit you should, look at renegotiating your outside laboratory costs, reducing the cost of supplies for in-house use, and increasing your fees.

To better understand if your laboratory income is in line with your laboratory expenses, see the graph on page 36. The markup is figured as the percentage increase in the cost of the service to arrive at a fee for the client. In other words, a test that costs the veterinarian $5.00 and is sold to the client at $10.00 has a 100% markup.

Significant Findings

The U.S. median is 11.9%. Medians and averages are all very close, which signifies that very few practices have laboratory incomes significantly higher or significantly lower than the median.

Feline practices have significantly more gross income derived from laboratory services than other practices, and mixed practices are 3 percentage points behind small animal practices. Laboratory income seems to be fairly consistent among the regions except the Pacific Northwest, which shows a median of 8.9%.

In addition, laboratory income is consistent across all practices as segmented by number of veterinarians. The segmentation by cost-of-living index shows no relationship between cost-of-living and laboratory income.

There does seem to be a correlation between amount of gross income and laboratory income as a percentage of gross income. Practices with a gross income of <$250,000 derive 10.0% of their gross income from laboratory income, while practices with $1,000,000+ in gross income have a laboratory income of 12.3%. Most likely, this contributes to the larger practices having higher average transaction charges (see page 30).

The median markup on laboratory services is 350%. The markup on laboratory services decreases as the cost of living increases (from 485% markup in low COL states to 326% in high COL states). This trend suggests that practices are increasing their laboratory fees at a rate slower than the rate of inflation.

RADIOLOGY INCOME AS A PERCENTAGE OF GROSS INCOME

General Overview	25th Percentile	Median	Average	75th Percentile	Number of Responses
U.S. Total (Mixed and Small)	2.1%	2.9%	3.1%	3.8%	525
Mixed Practices	1.6%	2.4%	2.6%	3.1%	108
Small Animal Practices	2.2%	2.9%	3.2%	3.8%	428
Feline Practices	1.8%	3.0%	3.0%	4.0%	19
Emergency/Critical Care Practices	3.8%	7.6%	7.5%	10.6%	25
Canada Total	1.8%	2.4%	2.8%	3.4%	40
Segmented by Region					
New England	2.3%	2.8%	3.0%	3.3%	28
Mid-Atlantic	2.2%	3.0%	3.2%	3.8%	52
South	1.6%	2.3%	2.4%	3.0%	69
Great Lakes	2.0%	2.8%	2.9%	3.5%	109
Plains	2.1%	2.9%	2.7%	3.5%	43
Northern Mountains	1.8%	3.0%	3.3%	5.6%	6
West	1.6%	2.6%	3.0%	4.0%	60
Pacific Northwest	2.3%	3.1%	3.4%	4.4%	22
Southwest	3.1%	3.8%	3.9%	4.4%	26
South Atlantic	1.8%	2.3%	2.4%	2.9%	49
Northern California	3.2%	4.5%	4.8%	6.4%	24
Southern California	3.4%	4.4%	4.4%	5.2%	18
Segmented by Number of Veterinarians					
1 Veterinarian	1.5%	2.2%	2.7%	3.2%	105
1.1–3 Veterinarians	2.0%	2.7%	2.8%	3.5%	245
3.1–5 Veterinarians	2.3%	2.9%	3.1%	3.7%	146
5+ Veterinarians	2.5%	3.5%	3.8%	5.0%	30
Segmented by Gross Income					
< $250,000 Gross Income	1.5%	2.3%	2.7%	3.2%	38
$250,000–$500,000 Gross Income	1.6%	2.2%	2.5%	3.2%	143
$500,000–$750,000 Gross Income	2.0%	2.6%	2.7%	3.4%	158
$750,000–$1,000,000 Gross Income	2.1%	2.7%	2.9%	3.5%	94
$1,000,000+ Gross Income	2.8%	3.2%	3.7%	4.7%	89
Segmented by Cost-of-Living Indices					
Low Cost-of-Living States	1.8%	2.4%	2.6%	3.1%	166
Average Cost-of-Living States	2.0%	2.9%	2.9%	3.8%	198
High Cost-of-Living States	2.7%	3.3%	3.8%	4.7%	125

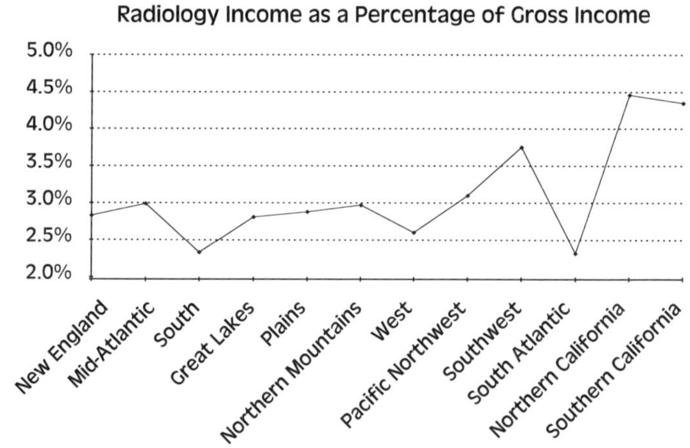

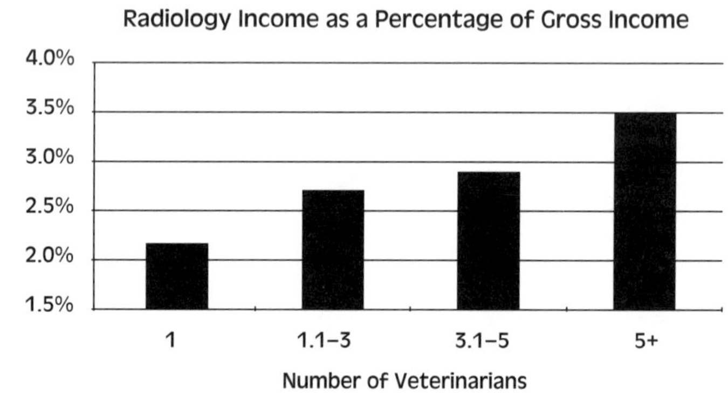

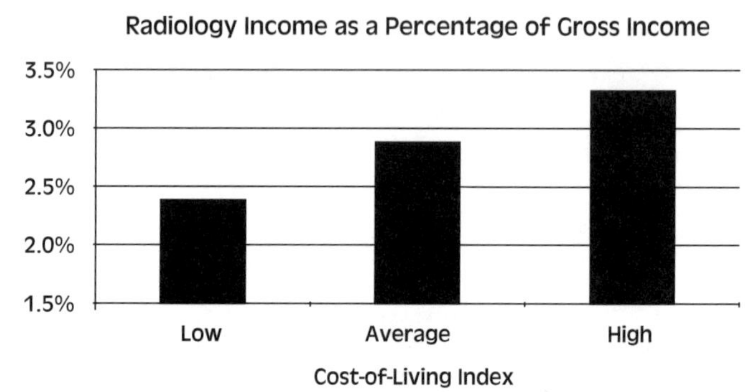

Radiology Income as a Percentage of Gross Income

Definition

Radiology income is a measure of the volume of services you provide in this area, including ultrasound income, and the fees you charge.

Examples of commonly missed opportunities in radiology income are:

- Building into the radiology estimate the need for multiple views or exposures
- Building processing and technician time into your fee structure

Significant Findings

The median practice in the United States derives 2.9% of its income from radiology services. Mixed practices have lower income in this area than do small animal practices. Except for the Northern California and Northern Mountains regions, the highest regional 75th percentile value is 5.2% (Southern California).

As the number of veterinarians and the gross income grow, so does the percentage of gross income from radiology.

While there is no correlation between laboratory income and the COL index, there seems to be a correlation between cost of living and the percentage of gross income derived from radiology services.

Note that practices in both Northern and Southern California have the highest median radiology income levels nationally. This is due in part to this state being on the cutting edge of radiation therapy for cancer patients as well as having clients who are willing to pay for those services.

DENTISTRY INCOME AS A PERCENTAGE OF GROSS INCOME

General Overview	25th Percentile	Median	Average	75th Percentile	Number of Responses
U.S. Total (Mixed and Small)	1.0%	1.5%	1.9%	2.3%	516
Mixed Practices	0.8%	1.2%	1.6%	1.8%	106
Small Animal Practices	1.0%	1.6%	2.0%	2.5%	422
Feline Practices	2.8%	3.1%	3.6%	3.8%	19
Canada Total	1.3%	1.7%	2.2%	2.7%	38
Segmented by Region					
New England	0.9%	1.2%	1.7%	2.0%	27
Mid-Atlantic	0.8%	1.0%	1.4%	1.9%	51
South	0.9%	1.2%	1.5%	1.9%	64
Great Lakes	0.9%	1.3%	1.9%	2.2%	108
Plains	1.1%	1.6%	1.7%	2.2%	43
Northern Mountains	1.5%	1.7%	1.8%	2.5%	6
West	1.3%	2.3%	2.9%	2.9%	58
Pacific Northwest	1.4%	2.1%	2.1%	2.6%	24
Southwest	1.3%	1.8%	2.2%	2.4%	26
South Atlantic	0.9%	1.4%	1.7%	1.9%	46
Northern California	1.2%	2.2%	2.3%	3.3%	24
Southern California	1.1%	2.0%	2.0%	2.3%	18
Segmented by Number of Veterinarians					
1 Veterinarian	1.0%	1.6%	2.4%	2.9%	105
1.1–3 Veterinarians	1.1%	1.7%	2.1%	2.5%	241
3.1–5 Veterinarians	1.0%	1.5%	1.8%	2.2%	141
5+ Veterinarians	0.8%	1.2%	1.4%	1.7%	29
Segmented by Gross Income					
< $250,000 Gross Income	1.1%	1.8%	2.1%	2.7%	38
$250,000–$500,000 Gross Income	1.0%	1.6%	2.0%	2.4%	141
$500,000–$750,000 Gross Income	1.1%	1.7%	2.3%	2.4%	153
$750,000–$1,000,000 Gross Income	1.0%	1.5%	1.9%	2.5%	93
$1,000,000+ Gross Income	0.9%	1.3%	1.6%	2.0%	87
Segmented by Cost-of-Living Indices					
Low Cost-of-Living States	0.9%	1.4%	1.9%	2.2%	161
Average Cost-of-Living States	1.0%	1.5%	1.9%	2.3%	194
High Cost-of-Living States	1.1%	1.6%	1.9%	2.4%	124

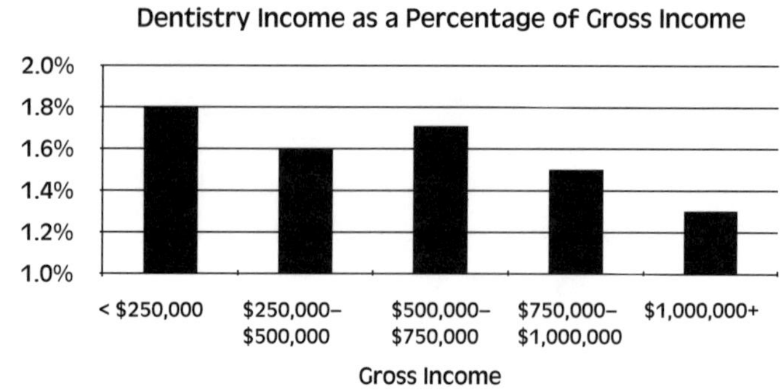

Dentistry Income as a Percentage of Gross Income

Definition

The percentage of gross income derived from dentistry shows you if you may be missing opportunities in dental client education and dentistry fees.

Examples of commonly missed opportunities in dentistry are:

- Checking the teeth every time you examine a pet
- Recommending dental services to the client
- Scheduling an appointment before the client leaves the practice
- Mailing dental reminders
- Promoting one or two dental months each year
- Distributing pamphlets or flyers that discuss basic dental care
- Training your technicians to do cleaning, scaling, and polishing
- Charging separately for each tooth extraction

Significant Findings

Dentistry income comprises a very small portion of a practice's annual gross income, with the U.S. median being 1.5%.

The data shows a very uniform average across the country with the exception of feline practices. In other words, practices have roughly the same percentage of dentistry income regardless of their size, location, and number of veterinarians. However, the West, Pacific Northwest, and Northern and Southern California regions all have higher dentistry income than the other regions.

Note that practices with a gross income of $1,000,000+ and practices with 5+ veterinarians have the lowest dentistry income percentages out of all of the practices surveyed. Practices with a gross income of <$250,000 have the highest dental income percentage. This trend suggests that as a practice grows, it does not maintain the same focus on dentistry and the related client education.

ANCILLARY SERVICES INCOME AS A PERCENTAGE OF GROSS INCOME

General Overview	25th Percentile	Median	Average	75th Percentile	Number of Responses
U.S. Total (Mixed and Small)	7.2%	13.3%	15.0%	21.3%	451
Mixed Practices	7.0%	12.6%	14.0%	18.7%	87
Small Animal Practices	7.7%	13.5%	15.2%	21.5%	376
Feline Practices	10.7%	15.5%	16.5%	20.8%	19
Canada Total	7.6%	14.2%	15.7%	22.5%	38
Segmented by Region					
New England	9.4%	16.9%	17.1%	21.3%	23
Mid-Atlantic	5.7%	13.3%	14.9%	25.6%	46
South	10.0%	12.6%	14.5%	18.5%	57
Great Lakes	5.7%	10.9%	12.7%	17.1%	102
Plains	10.6%	14.5%	16.1%	21.9%	37
Northern Mountains	6.7%	12.3%	16.3%	25.6%	5
West	6.6%	13.4%	14.3%	21.4%	50
Pacific Northwest	9.4%	17.6%	15.5%	18.8%	20
Southwest	9.8%	12.9%	14.2%	19.4%	24
South Atlantic	6.7%	17.8%	17.6%	25.4%	37
Northern California	9.9%	12.3%	14.7%	21.5%	19
Southern California	7.7%	10.3%	17.8%	30.1%	15
Segmented by Number of Veterinarians					
1 Veterinarian	8.7%	13.2%	14.5%	19.7%	91
1.1–3 Veterinarians	9.3%	14.0%	15.5%	21.6%	205
3.1–5 Veterinarians	7.0%	12.5%	14.8%	22.1%	128
5+ Veterinarians	5.8%	12.2%	13.7%	17.9%	30
Segmented by Gross Income					
< $250,000 Gross Income	9.7%	13.6%	16.4%	22.5%	35
$250,000–$500,000 Gross Income	9.3%	14.1%	15.8%	22.5%	117
$500,000–$750,000 Gross Income	6.2%	12.4%	13.4%	18.5%	137
$750,000–$1,000,000 Gross Income	8.8%	14.0%	15.1%	19.8%	84
$1,000,000+ Gross Income	6.2%	13.5%	15.7%	23.5%	75
Segmented by Cost-of-Living Indices					
Low Cost-of-Living States	8.2%	14.8%	15.8%	21.5%	135
Average Cost-of-Living States	5.8%	12.0%	13.4%	18.6%	177
High Cost-of-Living States	8.4%	16.4%	16.1%	21.5%	109

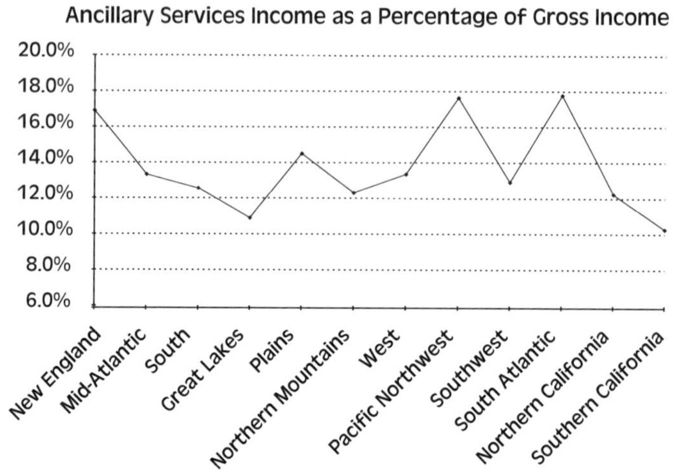

Ancillary Services Income as a Percentage of Gross Income

Definition

Ancillary services income includes income from boarding, grooming, over-the-counter sales of products and food, and prescription diet products. This percentage varies widely depending on the volume and mix of products and services provided.

You also need to examine how your markup on ancillary services compares to the median of 200% (see page 38 for ancillary services expenses and ancillary markups). Remember that this markup percentage includes the markup on food, which is typically around 30%, as well as boarding services, which may have a markup of 400%. Profit does not include any allocation for cost of shelf space or staff time involved, so it is not a true profit picture. However, it does give you a good idea of where you stand compared to others.

Ancillary services are just that, services other than your core business. If you approach these services with that in mind, you may want to concentrate on services with higher markups that fall in the clinical and medical arena (laboratory, pharmacy, and surgery income). However, this is not to say that ancillary services are not profitable. It is also not to say that these services do not attract new clients to the practice or keep existing clients happy. Therefore, you need to examine the profitability of various products and services individually.

Significant Findings

The ancillary services income data point has the largest variance nationally of all income segments tracked. The South Atlantic region is the highest, with a median of 17.8%; Southern California has the lowest median with 10.3%. The U.S. median is 13.3%. Eight out of 12 regions have a 75th percentile value of over 20%.

Because ancillary services include retail, food, and small-ticket items, they typically decrease a practice's ATC and increase its number of transactions per veterinarian.

You can see how ancillary services affect the practice as a whole when you examine practices in the South Atlantic region. These practices have the highest median ancillary services income percentage, the highest median number of transactions per veterinarian (see page 28), and the lowest median ATC nationally (see page 30).

There appears to be no relationship between practice size (in terms of the number of veterinarians or in terms of gross income) and the percentage of gross income derived from ancillary services.

Productivity

INCOME PER VETERINARIAN

General Overview	25th Percentile	Median	Average	75th Percentile	Number of Responses
U.S. Total (Mixed and Small)	$236,455	$279,284	$290,594	$327,807	581
Mixed Practices	$212,382	$268,776	$268,785	$306,750	126
Small Animal Practices	$242,521	$281,399	$297,261	$333,428	466
Feline Practices	$245,227	$308,075	$299,793	$375,000	19
Emergency/Critical Care Practices	$197,017	$235,437	$245,225	$280,791	23
Canada Total (in Canadian dollars)	$224,876	$270,717	$276,547	$292,778	43
Segmented by Region					
New England	$241,884	$311,322	$296,674	$333,321	32
Mid-Atlantic	$253,542	$280,741	$302,203	$328,669	55
South	$216,240	$279,284	$280,814	$317,979	76
Great Lakes	$228,766	$257,803	$268,788	$320,515	117
Plains	$208,193	$252,517	$250,849	$296,062	48
Northern Mountains	$233,022	$237,347	$287,488	$290,010	6
West	$216,875	$276,461	$270,806	$311,579	63
Pacific Northwest	$227,069	$270,185	$275,841	$284,240	29
Southwest	$268,776	$312,632	$337,789	$346,000	28
South Atlantic	$245,154	$294,645	$304,771	$358,364	57
Northern California	$280,813	$319,369	$339,126	$420,417	28
Southern California	$242,000	$380,157	$356,417	$456,015	21
Segmented by Number of Veterinarians					
1 Veterinarian	$208,140	$297,192	$310,418	$383,336	114
1.1–3 Veterinarians	$241,247	$296,062	$305,386	$348,280	274
3.1–5 Veterinarians	$227,069	$267,750	$275,075	$312,632	162
5+ Veterinarians	$256,547	$280,813	$284,460	$309,890	34
Segmented by Gross Income					
< $250,000 Gross Income	$130,000	$171,851	$166,225	$204,547	44
$250,000–$500,000 Gross Income	$209,637	$251,055	$262,354	$311,322	155
$500,000–$750,000 Gross Income	$222,575	$275,057	$283,946	$323,000	169
$750,000–$1,000,000 Gross Income	$240,968	$279,284	$296,782	$326,663	105
$1,000,000+ Gross Income	$269,028	$302,278	$322,065	$349,413	103
Segmented by Cost-of-Living Indices					
Low Cost-of-Living States	$231,576	$273,113	$278,614	$317,979	181
Average Cost-of-Living States	$231,959	$274,000	$281,744	$323,000	217
High Cost-of-Living States	$243,133	$284,240	$306,547	$368,800	143

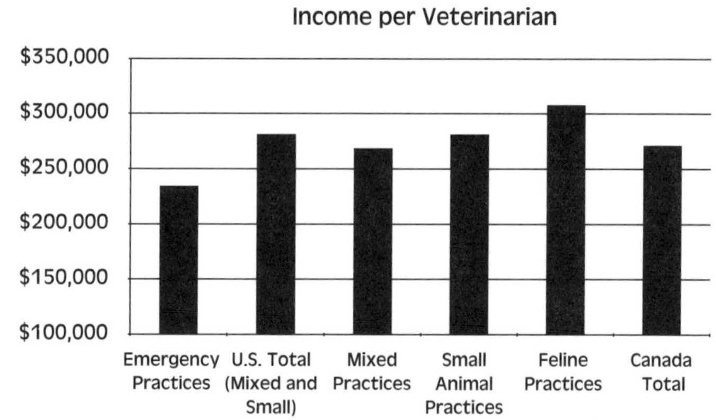

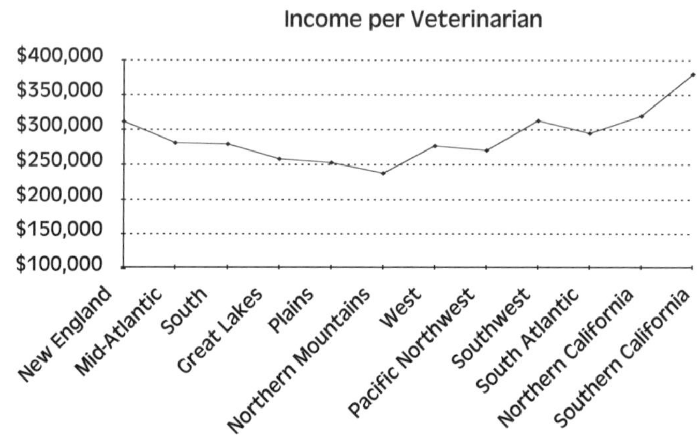

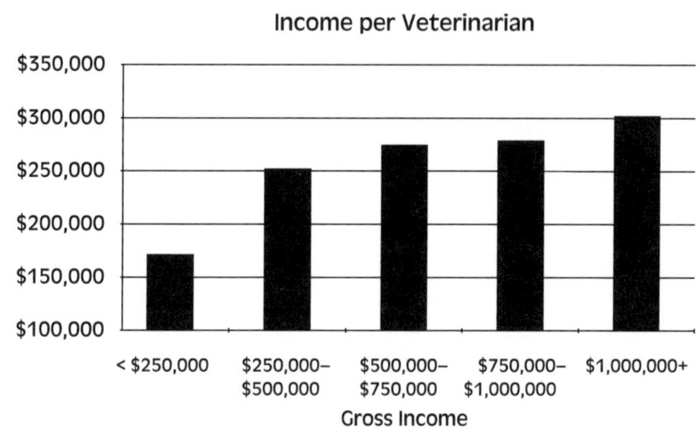

Income per Veterinarian

Definition

To calculate your income per veterinarian, divide your practice's gross income by the number of full-time equivalent veterinarians. *Income per veterinarian does not reflect personal production.* However, because we show each practice's gross income in terms of this productivity measure, you can draw some conclusions about how you stack up.

If your income per veterinarian is significantly lower than the median, research why. First, look at your ATC. Next, see if your transactions per veterinarian are too low. Low ATCs, low transaction numbers, or a combination may cause the income per veterinarian figure to be lower than ideal. Read the descriptions for the ATC (see page 31) and transactions per veterinarian (see page 29) to get a better idea of how to improve in these areas.

If your income per veterinarian is significantly higher than the U.S. median, it may be time to start thinking about hiring an associate. Once you reach a certain production plateau, which is different for each practice, it may be next to impossible to grow without adding another veterinarian. In addition, you may be so busy seeing a large volume of patients that your ATC suffers because you do not have enough time to offer and explain all treatment options. The quality of service may suffer as well.

Unfortunately, there is no magic number that represents the point at which you must hire an associate veterinarian. It depends on how many hours the owners want to work, how busy the practice is, how much space there is to grow, and many other factors. If the owners want to spend more time outside the practice and the income per veterinarian number is at or a little above the U.S. median, owners typically must be willing to decrease their compensation in order to buy that extra time.

Significant Findings

The median income per veterinarian in small animal practices is $281,399. In order to understand what is behind this number, you must analyze the ATC (see page 30) and the number of transactions per veterinarian (see page 28) figures—a more complete picture emerges when you do so.

Let's look at the U.S. region with the highest income per veterinarian: Southern California. Southern California has a high number of transactions per veterinarian (see page 28), but is not the highest (South Atlantic is higher and New England is about the same). So if veterinarians in those other regions have about the same or more transactions per veterinarian, why is Southern California the highest when it comes to income per veterinarian? The answer lies in the ATC (see page 30). Southern California's is near the top and second only to Northern California. High ATCs in combination with a high number of transactions per veterinarian make Southern California a winner. You should complete a similar analysis for your practice to understand why it compares favorably or unfavorably to other practices.

The data as segmented by the number of veterinarians show that income per veterinarian does not significantly increase as practices add more veterinarians. In fact, there is a slight dip in both the U.S. median and the average for practices with 3.1–5 veterinarians.

It is interesting to note that there is no pattern in income per veterinarian as the number of veterinarians increases. This means that in general, adding veterinarians doesn't necessarily equate to higher productivity levels.

Adding a veterinarian increases the practice's gross income (see pages 10 and 11), but it does not mean additional productivity in terms of dollars earned per veterinarian or additional profit as a percentage of gross income (see page 24). Though your net income does not increase as a percentage of gross income as the number of veterinarians increases, the net income does increase in terms of dollars. This is because you get the same percentage, but of a bigger gross income.

The data as segmented by gross income seems to show that the income per veterinarian increases as gross income increases. However, this is a trap in interpreting the data, because you should actually look at this relationship the other way around (i.e., the gross income increases because the veterinarians are producing more). Why does this happen? In general, both the ATC and the transactions per veterinarian increase as gross income increases (see pages 30 and 28), which positively affect income per veterinarian and the overall gross income.

You see that to get a higher gross income, a practice must not just add veterinarians but it must hire highly productive veterinarians.

NUMBER OF TRANSACTIONS PER VETERINARIAN

General Overview	25th Percentile	Median	Average	75th Percentile	Number of Responses
U.S. Total (Mixed and Small)	3,645	4,634	4,677	5,495	466
Mixed Practices	3,518	4,026	4,432	5,280	96
Small Animal Practices	3,668	4,770	4,743	5,553	381
Feline Practices	3,199	3,988	4,100	4,814	17
Emergency/Critical Care Practices	1,350	2,044	2,187	2,687	21
Canada Total	3,239	4,042	4,217	4,498	35
Segmented by Region					
New England	3,889	4,905	5,177	6,249	23
Mid-Atlantic	3,870	4,521	4,715	5,598	43
South	4,011	4,862	4,874	5,650	58
Great Lakes	3,298	4,180	4,523	5,453	98
Plains	3,265	4,129	4,157	4,959	42
Northern Mountains	4,059	4,792	4,394	5,054	4
West	3,365	4,570	4,466	5,079	48
Pacific Northwest	2,616	3,885	4,316	5,354	21
Southwest	3,755	4,614	4,700	5,316	27
South Atlantic	3,853	5,133	5,151	6,188	43
Northern California	3,577	4,780	4,667	5,500	20
Southern California	3,464	5,086	4,984	5,895	18
Segmented by Number of Veterinarians					
1 Veterinarian	3,885	5,012	5,362	6,905	82
1.1–3 Veterinarians	3,923	4,806	4,893	5,564	220
3.1–5 Veterinarians	3,526	4,455	4,525	5,373	136
5+ Veterinarians	3,445	3,889	4,225	5,079	31
Segmented by Gross Income					
< $250,000 Gross Income	2,648	3,582	3,562	4,398	34
$250,000–$500,000 Gross Income	3,585	4,566	4,725	5,503	121
$500,000–$750,000 Gross Income	3,526	4,526	4,629	5,313	139
$750,000–$1,000,000 Gross Income	3,870	4,815	4,794	5,451	84
$1,000,000+ Gross Income	3,755	4,780	4,733	5,598	86
Segmented by Cost-of-Living Indices					
Low Cost-of-Living States	3,807	4,777	4,796	5,650	142
Average Cost-of-Living States	3,461	4,595	4,538	5,373	177
High Cost-of-Living States	3,546	4,565	4,705	5,527	112

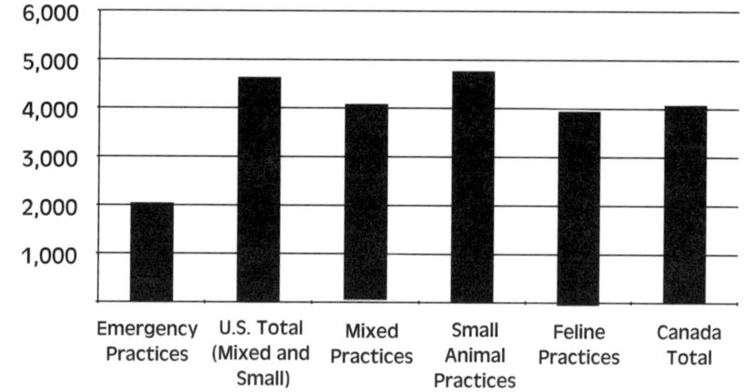

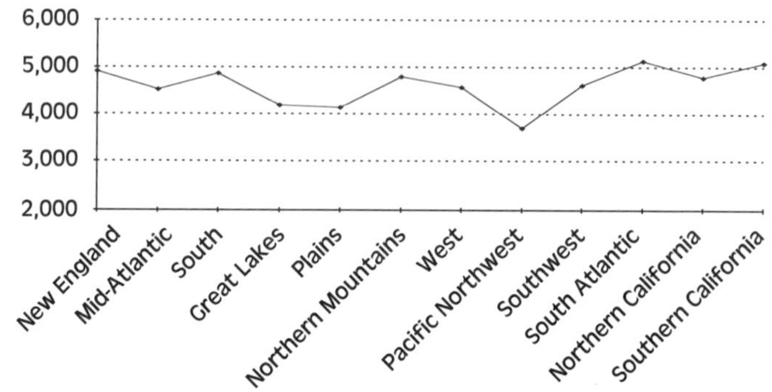

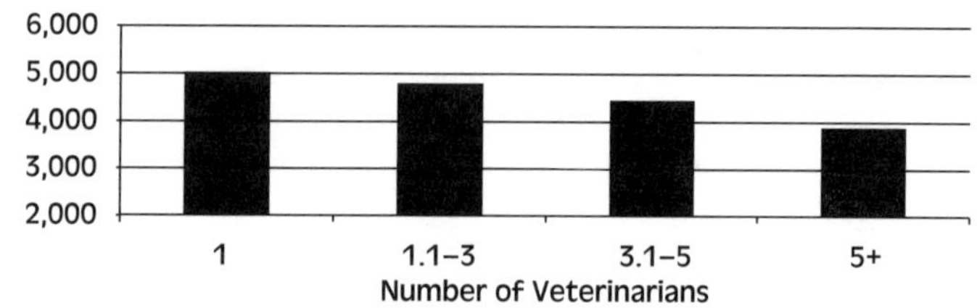

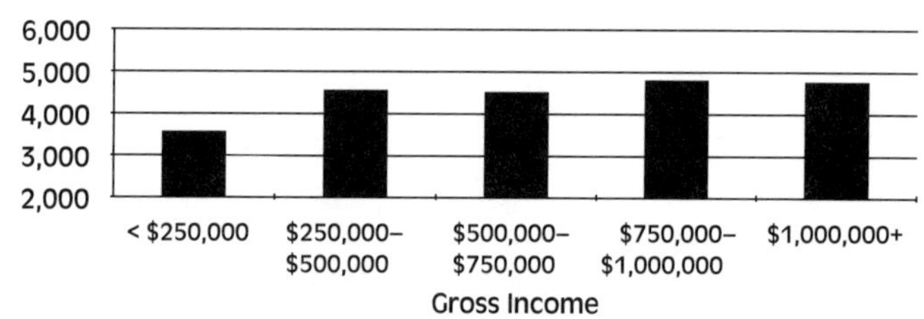

Number of Transactions per Veterinarian

Definition

The number of transactions per veterinarian is an indicator of your active client base, how many times per year your clients visit the practice, and how many new clients visit the practice. This measure of productivity, in combination with the average transaction charge, shows you where you should focus in order to increase gross income.

Transactions are defined as invoices, not as line items on invoices. Therefore, one invoice is generated for a client who comes in to purchase one bag of dog food and one invoice is generated for a multi-day hospital stay.

To increase the number of transactions per veterinarian, you may need to do the following:

- Build a more effective reminder system
- Follow up by phone after providing services to book recheck appointments or appointments to resolve a continuing problem
- Offer new services
- Make sure each client is aware of all the services you provide
- Use an effective marketing plan that addresses both existing and potential clients

Significant Findings

Small animal practices in the United States have a median number of transactions per veterinarian of 4,770, while mixed practices show a median of 4,026.

The data segmented by the number of veterinarians shows a definite pattern: As the number of veterinarians increases, the number of transactions per veterinarian decreases. However, the median average transaction charge increases as the number of veterinarians increases (see page 30), and they usually offset each other. Higher ATCs usually mean the veterinarian is spending more time on each appointment—more time translates into higher ATCs since the veterinarian is explaining and offering more treatment options, products, and services.

The one exception to the pattern is practices in the 3.1–5 veterinarian range. These practices do show a slight dip in income per veterinarian (see page 24), which indicates that their ATCs are not high enough to compensate for the drop in transactions per veterinarian.

You can make only one distinct conclusion about the number of transactions per veterinarian in the data segmented by gross income. The conclusion is that the practices at the <$250,000 gross income level have significantly fewer transactions per veterinarian than other practices. This makes sense if these practices are start-ups in their first or second year of operation.

AVERAGE TRANSACTION CHARGE (ATC)

General Overview	25th Percentile	Median	Average	75th Percentile	Number of Responses
U.S. Total (Mixed and Small)	$51.35	$59.76	$62.45	$71.26	480
Mixed Practices	$48.83	$56.46	$61.07	$71.95	102
Small Animal Practices	$52.07	$60.42	$63.01	$71.26	389
Feline Practices	$61.47	$66.46	$72.77	$73.84	17
Emergency/Critical Care Practices	$71.32	$112.12	$111.63	$140.38	24
Canada Total (in Canadian dollars)	$56.47	$63.38	$65.01	$74.71	36
Segmented by Region					
New England	$49.83	$59.34	$60.47	$70.71	24
Mid-Atlantic	$56.47	$63.08	$66.79	$74.66	45
South	$48.83	$56.51	$57.21	$63.60	61
Great Lakes	$50.79	$57.18	$60.47	$66.82	100
Plains	$52.86	$55.91	$61.31	$66.38	43
Northern Mountains	$48.63	$56.18	$54.03	$57.39	4
West	$50.66	$57.79	$61.78	$73.51	47
Pacific Northwest	$49.32	$61.53	$64.20	$74.78	22
Southwest	$53.80	$62.71	$67.40	$73.56	28
South Atlantic	$46.81	$55.87	$56.78	$64.28	46
Northern California	$61.52	$73.44	$72.79	$84.84	20
Southern California	$65.56	$71.70	$72.09	$80.79	19
Segmented by Number of Veterinarians					
1 Veterinarian	$45.90	$53.26	$57.29	$66.63	87
1.1–3 Veterinarians	$50.79	$58.41	$61.86	$70.81	225
3.1–5 Veterinarians	$52.19	$60.39	$61.78	$68.60	139
5+ Veterinarians	$56.31	$70.71	$69.85	$80.84	30
Segmented by Gross Income					
< $250,000 Gross Income	$45.04	$52.39	$52.39	$54.96	37
$250,000–$500,000 Gross Income	$46.61	$54.56	$55.10	$62.71	123
$500,000–$750,000 Gross Income	$50.77	$58.57	$60.66	$68.40	144
$750,000–$1,000,000 Gross Income	$51.43	$62.37	$63.41	$71.95	85
$1,000,000+ Gross Income	$54.72	$63.60	$67.20	$75.50	89
Segmented by Cost-of-Living Indices					
Low Cost-of-Living States	$47.81	$55.17	$56.88	$62.59	147
Average Cost-of-Living States	$52.70	$60.42	$62.29	$69.22	182
High Cost-of-Living States	$52.19	$68.56	$67.08	$75.61	116

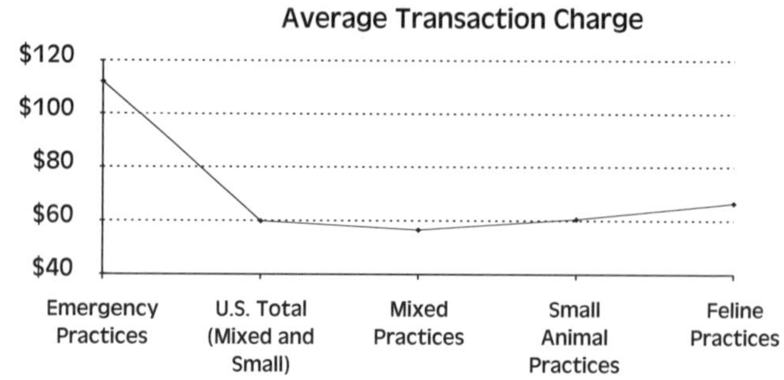

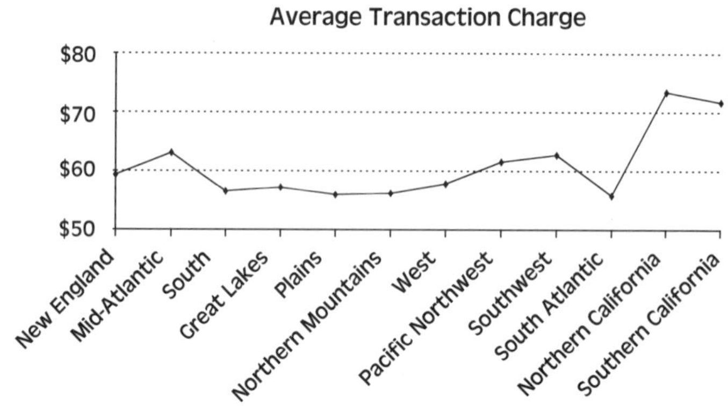

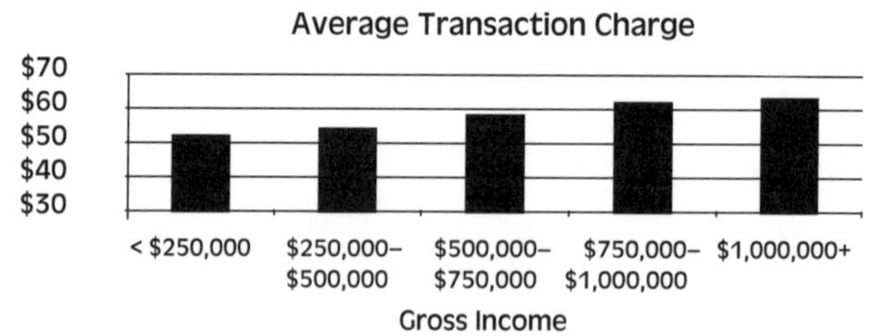

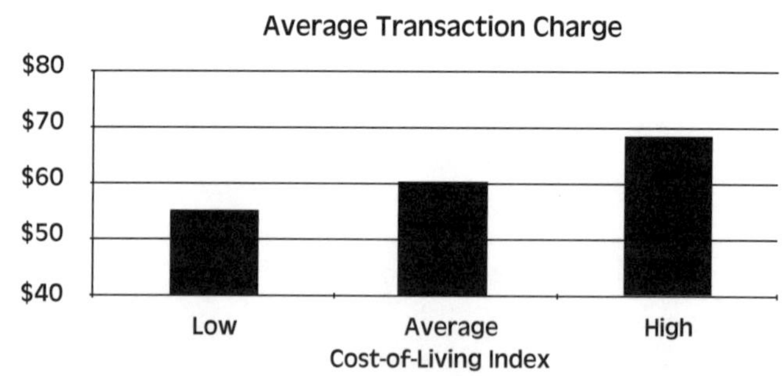

Average Transaction Charge (ATC)

Definition

This number tells you how much income per invoice you are billing. It is defined as gross income divided by the total number of transactions. A goal of every practice is to be profitable, and the ATC can be a significant factor contributing to a practice's success. By increasing the ATC by as little as $5, a practice grossing $600,000 and averaging 10,000 transactions per year can increase its gross income by 8.3%, or $50,000. Most of that increase falls directly to the bottom line.

Note: If your practice's ancillary services income percentage (see page 38) is much higher than the median, your ATC may be lower than the median. Practices that sell a high volume of ancillary products tend to have a higher-than-average number of low-dollar invoices: a bottle of shampoo here, a bag of dog food there. These low-dollar invoices reduce the overall ATC. (Ancillary services income includes income from boarding, grooming, over-the-counter sales of products and food, and prescription diet products.)

The following recommendations for increasing your ATC apply to any practice, not just those with lower-than-average ATCs:

1. Itemize and charge for every service you perform. For example, rechecks—even simple, quick ones—involve your time, your expertise, staff time, the staff's expertise, and facility expenses. Charge for these resources.
2. Offer all appropriate services to your clients. Treat the problem presented, but also make a sincere effort to care for the "whole pet." For example, a receptionist can pull the chart and see if the pet is overdue for a dental exam. The receptionist can suggest to the client that the doctor may recommend the service, the technician who does the check-in can reinforce the message, and the veterinarian can further emphasize how important the service is while in the exam room with the client. Offer to either complete the service that day or have the receptionist schedule the client for another time.
3. Be sure to enter the charges into the computer every time you perform a service for a hospitalized animal.
4. Evaluate the length of your clients' office visits. When you perform a puppy or kitten exam, do you take all of the time you need to explain *all* of the services that you provide? When a client brings in an adult pet with a problem, do you take the time you need to explain *all* treatment options? Making sure every client is aware of all the services you provide makes those clients more likely to use those services now and in the future. And don't be afraid to remind clients about your services on more than one visit. The typical person must hear the same message 5 to 10 times before it registers.
5. Complete laboratory and radiology work every time it is appropriate. Are you under-diagnosing? Compare your practice's gross income percentages for these categories to the regional medians for radiology and laboratory income percentages.
6. Don't be afraid to offer reassurance that the pet is healthy. For example, you may ask yourself why you should do a profile on a supposedly healthy animal. Clients are as conscious of wellness as they are of illness. The reassurance of a perfectly normal profile in an older pet is well worth the price to many people and many may perceive it as even more valuable if it uncovers hidden problems. And the baseline reference information is valuable for later comparisons.
7. Visit the best practice in your area (besides yours, of course) with a doctor/technician team from your own practice. What is that practice doing right? Observe how the practice is run and how it offers services to clients. You may get some excellent ideas you can apply in your own practice.
8. Question the dynamics of your staff and the level of staff buy-in. Does the staff really understand the importance of caring for the whole pet? Does the staff work with you to educate the clients? If not, what can you do to educate the staff first?

9. Examine your pricing structure. Is your fee structure based on your costs? Periodically calculate your expenses, including supplies, facility costs, and staff time for the more complex procedures and surgeries. Make sure your fees cover those costs and give you a reasonable profit. Remember: You typically won't encounter the same objections to prices for these services as you will for the "shopped" procedures like spays and declaws, so be sure to charge appropriately.
10. Re-evaluate all fees to make sure your fees are where they should be for your region. Refer to AAHA Press's *The Veterinary Fee Reference* for further information.
11. Charge different fees for different levels of office visits: basic, routine, expanded, and extensive. Set prices based on length of time and skill required.
12. Invest a little time and money to spruce up your waiting area and/or exam rooms. A coat of paint, new furniture, or some new wallpaper will change your clients' experience. You may see a large return on a small investment simply because the clients perceive a higher value than they did before.

Significant Findings

The U.S. median ATC is $59.76 with a 24% spread between the highest ATC at $73.44 (Northern California) and the lowest ATC at $55.87 (South Atlantic).

Though the percentage of gross income derived from ancillary services, laboratory, and radiology all have some impact on the ATC, no clear pattern within the regions proves a high correlation. What this means is that changing one factor, such as increasing laboratory income, will not necessarily have a huge impact on your ATC. Many factors work together, including your mix of products and services, how often you offer those services to clients, and your fees associated with such products and services.

In general, the ATC increases as the number of veterinarians increases. However, take into consideration that the number of transactions per veterinarian decreases as the number of veterinarians increases. Seeing fewer patients translates into more time with each patient, which translates into a higher ATC. Spending more time with clients most likely means you explain and offer more treatment options.

You will notice that an increasing ATC means increasing gross income. The way to more revenue is not through volume alone. Increasing your ATC is key, but keep in mind that the most effective way to increase profit is to increase both ATC *and* the number of transactions per veterinarian. How can you achieve that? Effectively use your staff to the fullest extent possible. Delegate tasks to your staff when possible, and reserve your time for seeing patients and doing surgery.

If you compare the low, average, and high COL states, you will notice that as the COL increases, the ATC also increases. This trend suggests that fees do correlate with the cost of living and that higher fees mean higher ATCs.

Mixed practices appear to have fewer transactions and lower ATCs per veterinarian (see pages 97 and 98) than their small animal counterparts. However, this does not necessarily translate into lower net income as a percentage of gross income for mixed practices (see page 97).

Expenses

DRUGS AND MEDICAL SUPPLIES EXPENSE AS A PERCENTAGE OF GROSS INCOME

General Overview	25th Percentile	Median	Average	75th Percentile	Number of Responses
U.S. Total (Mixed and Small)	12.4%	15.6%	15.9%	18.8%	530
Mixed Practices	15.5%	18.1%	18.5%	22.8%	101
Small Animal Practices	12.1%	14.8%	15.2%	18.0%	438
Feline Practices	7.2%	10.8%	11.6%	15.5%	17
Emergency/Critical Care Practices	8.3%	11.7%	11.5%	14.1%	28
Canada Total	10.5%	16.2%	16.7%	23.1%	40
Segmented by Region					
New England	13.9%	16.3%	16.2%	18.7%	31
Mid-Atlantic	10.5%	15.5%	14.8%	18.9%	54
South	15.2%	18.5%	18.6%	21.8%	64
Great Lakes	12.5%	14.7%	15.9%	18.3%	111
Plains	12.8%	14.4%	15.6%	18.1%	43
Northern Mountains	9.9%	10.0%	12.3%	11.8%	5
West	10.3%	14.1%	14.5%	17.8%	55
Pacific Northwest	13.3%	15.8%	17.2%	19.2%	27
Southwest	10.5%	12.2%	12.9%	15.3%	25
South Atlantic	13.2%	17.6%	17.2%	20.6%	50
Northern California	15.9%	16.7%	17.4%	20.5%	26
Southern California	9.9%	14.7%	13.8%	16.4%	21
Segmented by # of Veterinarians					
1 Veterinarian	14.5%	17.1%	17.7%	20.9%	95
1.1–3 Veterinarians	12.6%	15.7%	16.0%	18.7%	254
3.1–5 Veterinarians	12.5%	16.0%	16.2%	19.7%	151
5+ Veterinarians	10.3%	14.0%	14.0%	16.3%	30
Segmented by Gross Income					
< $250,000 Gross Income	14.2%	17.3%	16.9%	20.3%	35
$250,000–$500,000 Gross Income	14.2%	17.1%	17.3%	20.1%	148
$500,000–$750,000 Gross Income	14.1%	16.4%	17.0%	19.9%	152
$750,000–$1,000,000 Gross Income	13.1%	16.7%	16.7%	20.0%	95
$1,000,000+ Gross Income	10.3%	14.0%	14.0%	16.4%	97
Segmented by Cost-of-Living Indices					
Low Cost-of-Living States	13.4%	16.6%	16.7%	19.9%	160
Average Cost-of-Living States	12.1%	15.2%	15.5%	18.5%	200
High Cost-of-Living States	12.2%	15.9%	15.9%	18.2%	135

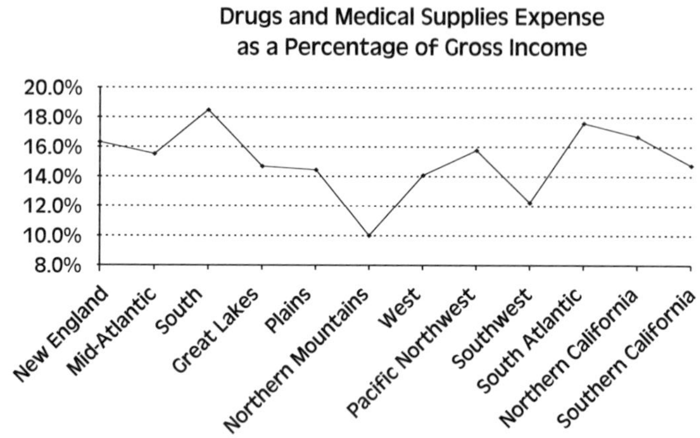

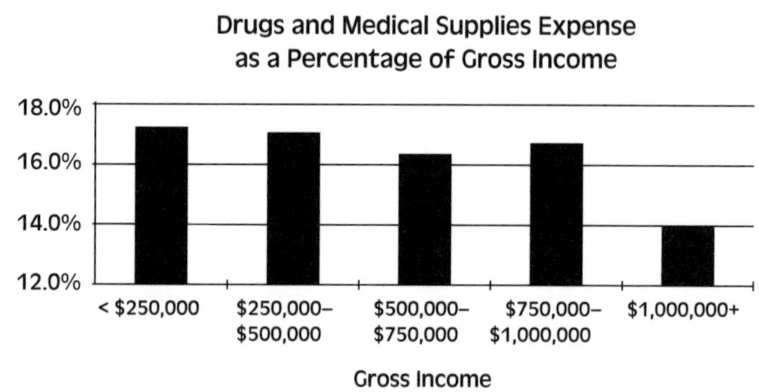

Drugs and Medical Supplies Expense as a Percentage of Gross Income

Definition

This expense includes all drugs and medical supplies, except any expenses involved with ancillary services and laboratory. (Ancillary services are boarding, grooming, sales of over-the-counter products and food, and prescription diet products.) They reflect how well you manage the inventory of drugs and medical supplies.

Are you spending more than the median? If so, you may be keeping too much money tied up in inventory. You should structure your inventory-ordering procedures so that you order as few supplies as possible without coming up short on an item you need. If you have excessively high drug expenses, try ordering smaller quantities more often. Avoid buying more than one brand of the same product. Also, shop around for the best prices, but do not spend more money on the staff time it takes to shop the best price than you can make up in the price difference; there is a point of diminishing return.

Be careful about accepting the offers of a year's supply of one item at a discount. Before making a decision to buy, be sure:

- You cannot use your shelf space more efficiently
- You can use the large quantity within 90 days
- You aren't tying up too much money in inventory when you could be earning interest on a short-term investment such as a certificate of deposit or reaching a financial goal.

Have only one person do the ordering. It is best to have someone other than the person who does the ordering check in the inventory when it arrives. Separating these duties helps to prevent theft.

If your drugs and medical supplies expense is significantly lower than the median, you do not have much to worry about other than having enough inventory in stock to meet both your clients' demands and your needs. You are likely doing a great job of keeping your inventory under control.

Significant Findings

Drugs and medical supplies expense as a percentage of gross income varies quite a bit depending on the type of practice and the region. The U.S. median is 15.6%, with feline practices having expenses of only 10.8% and mixed practices having a high of 18.1%. Feline practices are required to carry fewer drugs and supplies because they cater to only one species. Conversely, mixed practices cater to more species than small animal practices, so their drugs expense is much higher than the median.

There is some evidence that proves larger practices enjoy economies of scale. Practices with a gross income of <$250,000 have median drug expenses of 17.3%, while practices with a gross income of $1,000,000+ have a median of 14.0%. In addition, 1-veterinarian practices have a median of 17.1% and practices with 5+ veterinarians have median drug expenses of 14.0%. The drugs and medical supplies expense for practices at the far ends of the scales is quite different, but the values for those in the middle are all about the same.

LABORATORY EXPENSE AS A PERCENTAGE OF GROSS INCOME

General Overview	25th Percentile	Median	Average	75th Percentile	Number of Responses
U.S. Total (Mixed and Small)	1.6%	2.5%	2.6%	3.4%	544
Mixed Practices	1.4%	2.4%	2.4%	3.4%	116
Small Animal Practices	1.6%	2.6%	2.7%	3.5%	439
Feline Practices	2.5%	3.8%	3.8%	4.9%	18
Emergency/Critical Care Practices	1.2%	2.2%	2.5%	3.0%	24
Canada Total	1.4%	2.3%	2.3%	2.9%	38
Segmented by Region					
New England	1.4%	2.5%	2.5%	2.8%	30
Mid-Atlantic	1.9%	2.8%	2.8%	3.4%	53
South	1.2%	2.0%	2.4%	3.4%	73
Great Lakes	2.0%	2.7%	2.8%	3.6%	113
Plains	1.2%	2.3%	2.4%	3.7%	41
Northern Mountains	1.2%	2.6%	2.1%	2.6%	6
West	1.0%	2.2%	2.5%	3.8%	60
Pacific Northwest	1.7%	2.4%	2.4%	2.7%	26
Southwest	1.9%	2.5%	2.6%	3.7%	27
South Atlantic	1.0%	1.7%	1.8%	2.4%	50
Northern California	2.6%	3.0%	3.0%	3.6%	27
Southern California	2.7%	3.2%	3.4%	4.0%	19
Segmented by Number of Veterinarians					
1 Veterinarian	1.0%	1.9%	2.1%	3.0%	105
1.1–3 Veterinarians	1.6%	2.4%	2.5%	3.3%	255
3.1–5 Veterinarians	1.4%	2.5%	2.6%	3.3%	151
5+ Veterinarians	2.4%	2.8%	3.0%	3.6%	34
Segmented by Gross Income					
< $250,000 Gross Income	0.9%	1.9%	2.2%	3.3%	41
$250,000–$500,000 Gross Income	1.4%	2.4%	2.4%	3.2%	149
$500,000–$750,000 Gross Income	1.5%	2.3%	2.4%	3.2%	154
$750,000–$1,000,000 Gross Income	1.5%	2.5%	2.7%	3.3%	96
$1,000,000+ Gross Income	1.9%	2.7%	2.7%	3.6%	100
Segmented by Cost-of-Living Indices					
Low Cost-of-Living States	1.2%	2.0%	2.3%	3.2%	169
Average Cost-of-Living States	1.6%	2.4%	2.5%	3.4%	205
High Cost-of-Living States	2.2%	2.7%	2.9%	3.6%	132

Comparison of Ancillary Services Markup Versus Laboratory Markup

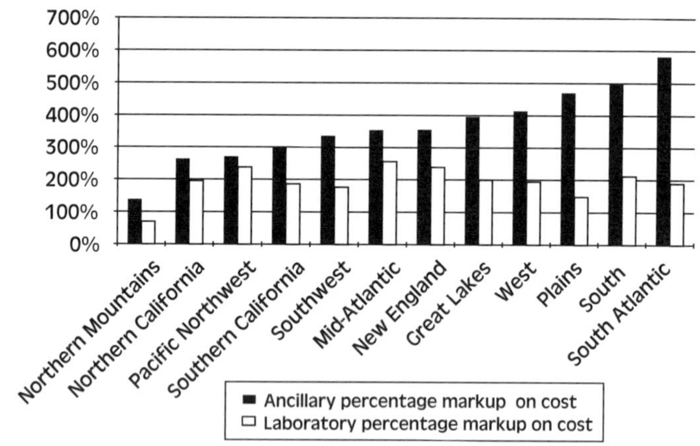

Percentage Markup on Laboratory Services

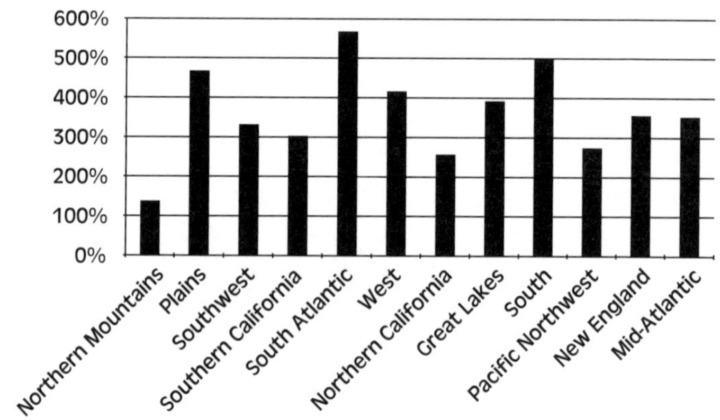

Percentage Markup on Laboratory Services

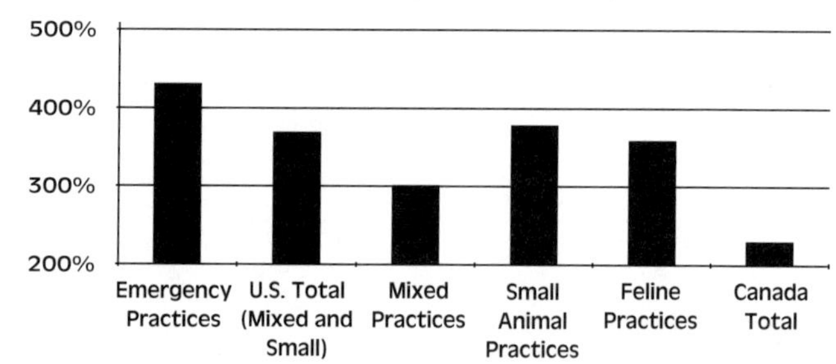

Laboratory Expense as a Percentage of Gross Income

Definition

Laboratory expense includes the cost of supplies used for in-house laboratory work and the cost of outside laboratory services. They do not include staff time or the cost of equipment.

Laboratory costs are hard to pin down as "too high" or "too low" because they depend on how much volume you have and on your fees. If your laboratory expense as a percentage of gross income is below 2%, you should take a look at how frequently you offer these services to your clients.

If your laboratory expense is high compared to the median, you may need to counteract high expenses by controlling your costs or raising fees. You may want to shop around to find the most competitive rates for outside laboratory services. A high laboratory expense figure could reflect a practice that does lots of laboratory work.

Also compare your laboratory markup to the graph on page 36. If your markup is low, you may need to control costs, increase fees, or both.

Significant Findings

The U.S. median laboratory expense is 2.5%, with most regions and practice types falling between 2% and 3%. There is not much variation, and only feline practices stand out as being significantly higher, with a median of 3.8% and a 75th percentile of 4.9%.

The fact that the medians are about the same for all regions signifies that laboratory expenses are extremely uniform. However, when you reference laboratory expense percentages against laboratory income (see page 14), it is obvious that various regions charge substantially different fees for laboratory services (see the range in markup percentages in the graph on page 36). This is confirmed in AAHA Press's *The Veterinary Fee Reference.*

Laboratory expense as a percentage of gross income differs depending on the practice size. One-veterinarian practices have laboratory expense of 1.9% and 5+ veterinarian practices have a laboratory expenses of 2.8%. There is a similar jump between practices with a gross income of <$250,000 and practices with a gross income of $1,000,000+. The markup, though, is much higher in the smaller practices (500% in 1-veterinarian practices and 311% in 5+ veterinarian practices).

Note that the states in the high COL areas have higher laboratory expenses than the low or average COL states, but have lower laboratory income than the low and average COL states (see page 14). This suggests that practices in high COL areas may not be marking up their laboratory services as much as they should be to compensate for higher costs.

The markup on laboratory services varies quite a bit, from a low of 138% in the Northern Mountains region to a high of 582% in the South Atlantic region (see page 36). The median markup on laboratory expenses is about 350%.

NOTE: The below-average markup percentage of 138% in the Northern Mountains region may result from the low number of respondents in this region.

ANCILLARY SERVICES EXPENSE AS A PERCENTAGE OF GROSS INCOME

General Overview	25th Percentile	Median	Average	75th Percentile	Number of Responses
U.S. Total (Mixed and Small)	2.7%	4.4%	4.9%	6.5%	424
Mixed Practices	2.4%	4.6%	4.8%	6.1%	85
Small Animal Practices	2.7%	4.5%	4.9%	6.6%	351
Feline Practices	5.6%	6.1%	7.4%	10.3%	15
Canada Total	4.1%	7.2%	7.4%	10.0%	25
Segmented by Region					
New England	4.0%	5.0%	6.0%	8.3%	21
Mid-Atlantic	2.4%	3.8%	4.6%	6.5%	45
South	2.6%	4.0%	4.2%	5.4%	53
Great Lakes	2.5%	3.6%	4.0%	5.1%	89
Plains	4.7%	5.9%	6.2%	7.6%	35
Northern Mountains	2.0%	7.3%	8.1%	13.2%	4
West	2.7%	4.5%	5.0%	7.1%	50
Pacific Northwest	2.7%	5.2%	4.6%	5.8%	18
Southwest	3.7%	4.7%	5.8%	7.3%	23
South Atlantic	3.6%	6.1%	6.2%	8.2%	36
Northern California	2.6%	4.2%	4.3%	5.8%	19
Southern California	2.4%	3.6%	4.9%	5.5%	13
Segmented by Number of Veterinarians					
1 Veterinarian	3.4%	4.7%	5.2%	6.6%	75
1.1–3 Veterinarians	3.1%	4.7%	5.2%	7.3%	202
3.1–5 Veterinarians	2.6%	4.3%	4.7%	6.1%	122
5+ Veterinarians	2.4%	3.7%	4.4%	5.5%	27
Segmented by Gross Income					
< $250,000 Gross Income	2.8%	5.1%	5.2%	7.1%	33
$250,000–$500,000 Gross Income	3.0%	5.2%	5.5%	7.3%	110
$500,000–$750,000 Gross Income	2.6%	4.0%	4.5%	5.9%	114
$750,000–$1,000,000 Gross Income	3.0%	4.1%	4.5%	6.0%	85
$1,000,000+ Gross Income	2.6%	5.0%	5.1%	7.1%	81
Segmented by Cost-of-Living Indices					
Low Cost-of-Living States	3.2%	4.8%	5.3%	7.3%	132
Average Cost-of-Living States	2.8%	4.5%	4.7%	6.5%	163
High Cost-of-Living States	2.5%	3.9%	4.5%	5.8%	98

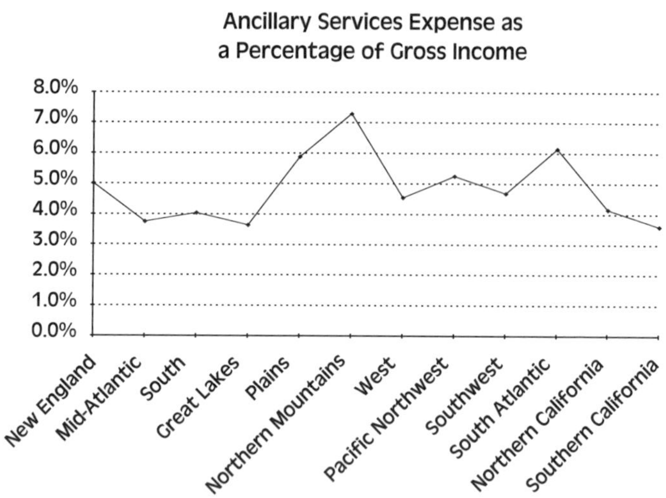

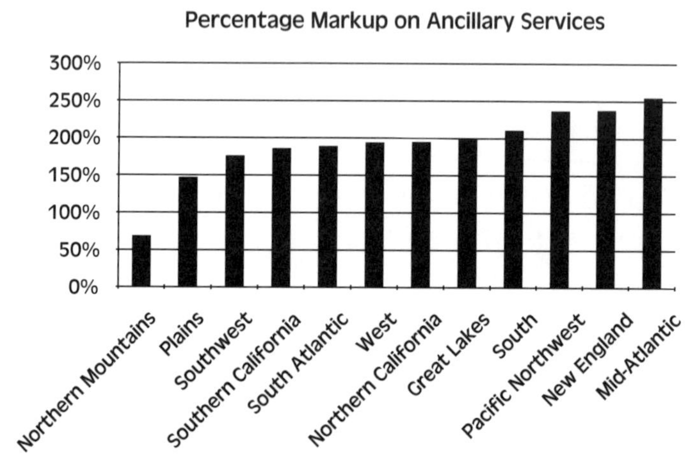

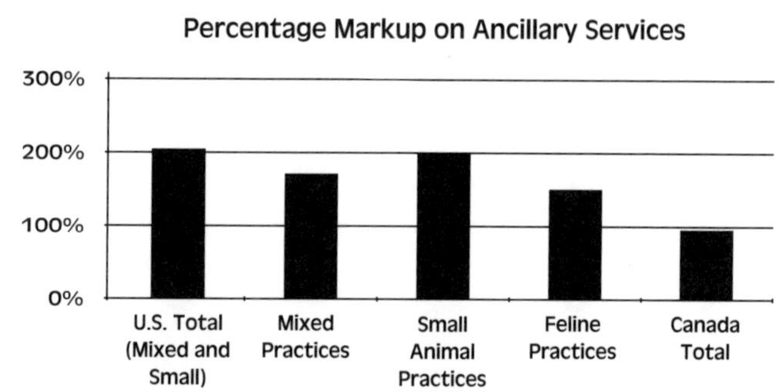

Ancillary Services Expense as a Percentage of Gross Income

Definition

Ancillary services expense includes costs associated with over-the-counter items such as leashes and collars, food, prescription food, boarding, and grooming. It does not include staff time or the cost of major equipment that is classified as an asset. Ancillary services expense can vary widely depending on the volume and types of products and services involved.

When you compare your markup percentages to those in the graph on page 38, be aware that the markup percentages can vary significantly from practice to practice due to the mix of products and services. (See the "Ancillary Services Income as a Percentage of Gross Income" section for a more detailed explanation of how to evaluate your profit margin.)

Significant Findings

The U.S. median ancillary services expense percentage is 4.4%.

The graph on page 38 shows the markup on ancillary services by region. It appears that ancillary services are generally marked up by about 200%. Remember that this number includes the markup on food, which is typically around 30%.

Practice size, whether in terms of the number of veterinarians or in terms of gross income, does not seem to make a difference when it comes to ancillary services expenses.

NOTE: The below-average markup percentage of 69% in the Northern Mountains region may be due to the low number of respondents.

ASSOCIATE VETERINARIANS SALARY EXPENSE AS A PERCENTAGE OF GROSS INCOME

General Overview	25th Percentile	Median	Average	75th Percentile	Number of Responses
U.S. Total (Mixed and Small)	5.9%	8.4%	8.9%	12.0%	441
Mixed Practices	5.7%	8.4%	8.7%	12.0%	93
Small Animal Practices	6.0%	8.3%	8.9%	11.9%	354
Feline Practices	3.3%	7.2%	6.8%	9.9%	11
Canada Total	4.5%	7.5%	7.5%	9.5%	33
Segmented by Region					
New England	4.3%	9.9%	9.2%	13.0%	26
Mid-Atlantic	6.6%	10.3%	10.4%	14.0%	47
South	7.0%	8.2%	8.6%	11.7%	53
Great Lakes	6.3%	10.0%	9.6%	12.8%	92
Plains	6.1%	8.1%	9.0%	12.3%	35
Northern Mountains	6.9%	6.9%	6.8%	6.9%	3
West	5.3%	7.2%	8.3%	10.7%	43
Pacific Northwest	4.9%	8.1%	7.9%	10.4%	22
Southwest	7.1%	10.4%	9.3%	12.5%	22
South Atlantic	5.6%	6.7%	7.3%	8.3%	44
Northern California	5.9%	6.1%	7.7%	12.4%	22
Southern California	4.4%	7.7%	8.2%	9.8%	17
Segmented by Number of Veterinarians					
1 Veterinarian	1.5%	2.4%	4.0%	5.0%	33
1.1–3 Veterinarians	5.7%	7.2%	7.9%	10.2%	234
3.1–5 Veterinarians	6.8%	9.9%	9.7%	12.8%	146
5+ Veterinarians	7.0%	9.7%	10.3%	13.0%	29
Segmented by Gross Income					
< $250,000 Gross Income	4.8%	6.1%	8.7%	12.7%	14
$250,000–$500,000 Gross Income	4.1%	6.0%	6.4%	8.9%	106
$500,000–$750,000 Gross Income	5.8%	7.9%	8.3%	10.8%	135
$750,000–$1,000,000 Gross Income	6.7%	9.9%	9.7%	13.0%	92
$1,000,000+ Gross Income	6.5%	9.2%	9.5%	12.8%	94
Segmented by Cost-of-Living Indices					
Low Cost-of-Living States	5.8%	7.4%	8.1%	10.1%	128
Average Cost-of-Living States	6.3%	9.2%	9.3%	12.6%	169
High Cost-of-Living States	5.9%	9.2%	9.1%	12.4%	114

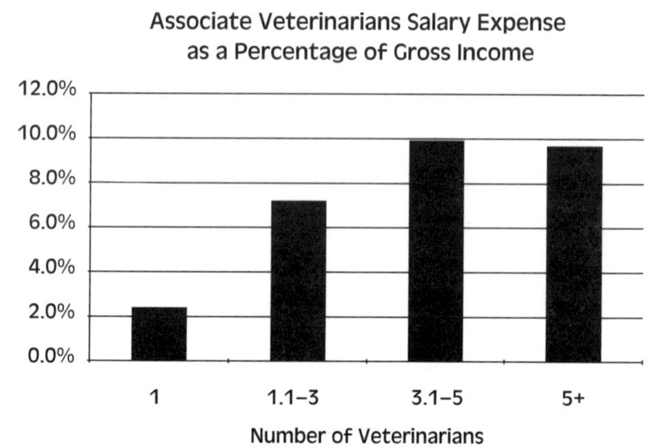

Associate Veterinarians Salary Expense as a Percentage of Gross Income

Definition

This is a measure of how much you are paying your associate veterinarians as a percentage of the practice's gross income, not as a percentage of the associate veterinarians' personal production.

There is no good or bad number here. Just make sure your compensation structure is fair and that owners are taking an appropriate amount of salary and profit out of the practice (see page 40).

Remember that the percentage of gross income you pay to associate veterinarians depends on how many owners and associate veterinarians are in the practice. For example, a practice with one owner and three associate veterinarians will have a much different expense than a practice with three owners and one associate veterinarian.

In some situations, you expect to pay a larger percentage to associate veterinarians than other practices do. For instance, if you go from working full-time to half-time, you may have to pay more in associate veterinarian compensation to "buy" the extra time off.

Significant Findings

The U.S. median associate veterinarians salary expense as a percentage of gross income is 8.4%. The highest value in the 75th percentile range is 14.0% for the Mid-Atlantic region.

One-veterinarian practices do show an expense for associate veterinarians, but this may be because some of those owners work less than full-time and have an associate veterinarian work part-time as well. It may also be due to a reporting error. Some 1-veterinarian practices may have reported the cost of relief veterinarians as an expense of associate veterinarians by mistake.

As expected, smaller practices have lower associate veterinarian expenses. One interesting point, though, is that this figure is about the same in practices in the 3.1–5 veterinarian range and in the 5+ veterinarian range. If a practice added associate veterinarians but kept the same number of owners as it grew, you would expect that practice to have higher associate veterinarians salary expense as a percentage of gross income than it did before. Instead, the cost as a percentage of gross income decreases slightly from the 3.1–5 range to the 5+ range. It seems that as practices grow, they pull one of the existing associate veterinarians into ownership and hire a new associate veterinarian in his or her place.

Note: There are tax ramifications for receiving owner compensation versus payments on ownership interest in a practice that complicate this situation.

There is a good discussion of related issues in AAHA Press's *Structuring an Associate Buy-In*.

NONVETERINARIAN STAFF SALARY EXPENSE AS A PERCENTAGE OF GROSS INCOME

General Overview	25th Percentile	Median	Average	75th Percentile	Number of Responses
U.S. Total (Mixed and Small)	17.7%	20.0%	20.4%	22.6%	411
Mixed Practices	17.4%	18.8%	19.8%	21.0%	79
Small Animal Practices	17.9%	20.0%	20.5%	23.0%	344
Feline Practices	17.2%	18.9%	20.7%	25.7%	17
Emergency/Critical Care Practices	16.4%	19.3%	20.0%	23.0%	28
Canada Total	16.9%	18.9%	19.8%	21.7%	32
Segmented by Region					
New England	20.3%	21.0%	21.4%	24.2%	20
Mid-Atlantic	17.4%	19.6%	20.5%	23.0%	40
South	18.0%	19.5%	20.0%	21.7%	57
Great Lakes	17.7%	20.0%	19.8%	21.3%	80
Plains	18.1%	19.2%	20.5%	23.1%	33
Northern Mountains	16.1%	20.7%	19.4%	20.7%	5
West	18.0%	21.0%	21.4%	24.1%	40
Pacific Northwest	16.2%	18.2%	19.9%	24.2%	19
Southwest	17.4%	18.6%	20.8%	26.3%	21
South Atlantic	17.7%	19.8%	20.2%	21.4%	44
Northern California	18.4%	20.6%	20.7%	22.0%	20
Southern California	17.4%	17.6%	19.1%	21.0%	18
Segmented by Number of Veterinarians					
1 Veterinarian	16.6%	18.6%	19.3%	20.7%	78
1.1–3 Veterinarians	17.9%	19.7%	20.4%	22.7%	193
3.1–5 Veterinarians	18.0%	20.0%	20.5%	22.4%	114
5+ Veterinarians	17.3%	20.7%	20.7%	24.0%	27
Segmented by Gross Income					
< $250,000 Gross Income	16.4%	19.4%	19.5%	20.6%	27
$250,000–$500,000 Gross Income	17.4%	19.5%	20.1%	22.3%	112
$500,000–$750,000 Gross Income	17.5%	19.3%	19.9%	21.4%	113
$750,000–$1,000,000 Gross Income	18.4%	19.5%	20.2%	21.3%	74
$1,000,000+ Gross Income	18.0%	20.7%	20.9%	24.0%	83
Segmented by Cost-of-Living Indices					
Low Cost-of-Living States	18.1%	20.0%	20.5%	23.0%	127
Average Cost-of-Living States	17.7%	19.6%	20.2%	21.6%	151
High Cost-of-Living States	17.6%	19.8%	20.5%	22.7%	105

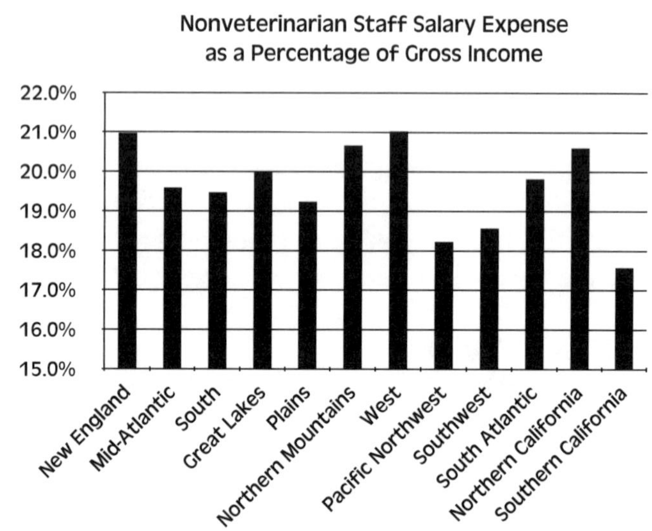

Nonveterinarian Staff Salary Expense as a Percentage of Gross Income

Definition

This is the money you spend on nonveterinarian staff, including the employer's portion of FICA, other payroll taxes, and bonuses. You should evaluate this number in conjunction with the nonveterinarian staff per veterinarian ratio (see page 6).

If your nonveterinarian staff salary expense is higher than the median for your practice size or practice type, you may:

- Have too many employees for your level of gross income
- Have a highly paid staff or a large number of staff in order to provide the level of service you desire in your practice
- Be paying more than the market rate in order to keep good employees
- Be less productive than the normal practice

If your nonveterinarian staff salary expense is lower than the median, you may:

- Have too few staff to support the practice
- Be underpaying your staff
- Be more productive than the average practice

Significant Findings

The U.S. median is 20.0%, and most regions are between 18% and 21%. Several regions have 75th percentile values of 24% and above.

While practices in the 1.1–5 veterinarian range do not seem to have very different nonveterinarian staff salary expense percentages, there is a 2 percentage point difference between 1-veterinarian practices and 5+ veterinarian practices (18.6% and 20.7%, respectively).

Interestingly enough, practices in the 5+ veterinarian range have the same number of nonveterinarian staff per veterinarian as 1-veterinarian practices (see page 6). Perhaps bigger practices want to or have to pay more for their staff because they require higher skill levels to support a higher volume of clients and to support more complex services.

EMPLOYEE BENEFITS PROGRAM EXPENSE AS A PERCENTAGE OF GROSS INCOME

General Overview	25th Percentile	Median	Average	75th Percentile	Number of Responses
U.S. Total (Mixed and Small)	1.1%	2.0%	2.3%	3.2%	436
Mixed Practices	1.1%	1.8%	2.1%	2.9%	97
Small Animal Practices	1.1%	2.0%	2.3%	3.2%	348
Feline Practices	0.9%	2.0%	2.3%	2.8%	14
Emergency/Critical Care Practices	1.6%	1.8%	2.4%	3.2%	22
Canada Total	0.7%	1.0%	1.6%	2.6%	28
Segmented by Region					
New England	1.9%	2.5%	2.7%	3.6%	25
Mid-Atlantic	1.3%	2.6%	2.5%	3.4%	45
South	1.1%	1.8%	2.1%	2.8%	56
Great Lakes	1.5%	2.4%	2.6%	3.8%	92
Plains	1.0%	1.7%	2.1%	3.2%	33
Northern Mountains	0.3%	1.7%	1.4%	2.1%	5
West	1.3%	2.4%	2.3%	2.9%	45
Pacific Northwest	1.2%	2.3%	2.4%	4.0%	21
Southwest	0.8%	1.1%	1.6%	2.6%	21
South Atlantic	0.7%	2.2%	2.2%	3.2%	38
Northern California	0.7%	1.1%	1.4%	2.0%	21
Southern California	1.4%	2.1%	2.8%	5.4%	15
Segmented by Number of Veterinarians					
1 Veterinarian	0.8%	1.8%	1.9%	2.8%	63
1.1–3 Veterinarians	0.9%	1.7%	2.1%	3.0%	213
3.1–5 Veterinarians	1.2%	2.1%	2.5%	3.5%	133
5+ Veterinarians	1.2%	2.3%	2.2%	3.0%	28
Segmented by Gross Income					
< $250,000 Gross Income	0.5%	1.2%	1.6%	2.0%	18
$250,000–$500,000 Gross Income	0.9%	1.6%	1.8%	2.4%	112
$500,000–$750,000 Gross Income	0.9%	1.8%	2.1%	2.8%	131
$750,000–$1,000,000 Gross Income	1.0%	1.9%	2.4%	3.9%	86
$1,000,000+ Gross Income	1.3%	2.3%	2.5%	3.2%	88
Segmented by Cost-of-Living Indices					
Low Cost-of-Living States	1.0%	1.8%	2.3%	3.2%	134
Average Cost-of-Living States	1.2%	2.3%	2.3%	3.2%	160
High Cost-of-Living States	1.1%	1.9%	2.3%	3.2%	106

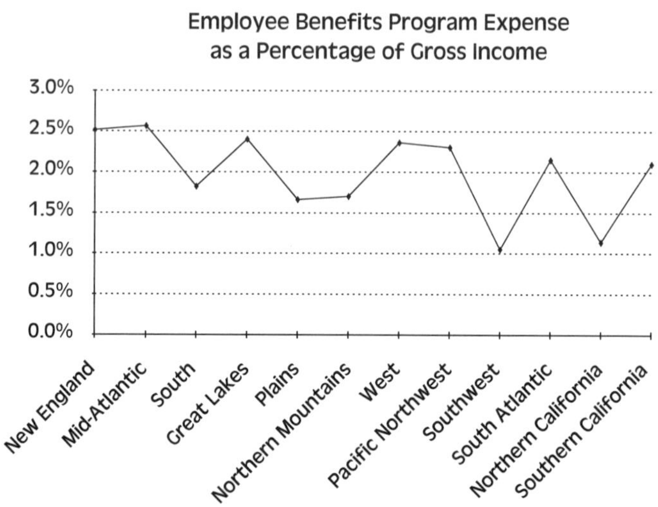

Employee Benefits Program Expense as a Percentage of Gross Income

Definition

Employee benefits vary from practice to practice. A higher-than-average percentage is not necessarily a red flag, but may simply mean you pay more in employee benefits because you either value staff or are "making up for" paying less than market value.

Significant Findings

The U.S. median for this expense is 2.0%, but the regions show a range between 1.1% and 2.6%. There is a difference between the smallest practices (<$250,000) and the largest practices ($1,000,000+), which spend 1.2% and 2.3% of their gross incomes on employee benefits, respectively. The discrepancy is most likely because smaller practices cannot afford to pay for more than the basic benefits. As practices' gross income increases, they have the luxury of providing more employee benefits.

RENT/LEASE OF FACILITY EXPENSE AS A PERCENTAGE OF GROSS INCOME

General Overview	25th Percentile	Median	Average	75th Percentile	Number of Responses
U.S. Total (Mixed and Small)	4.0%	5.7%	5.9%	7.7%	405
Mixed Practices	3.3%	5.3%	5.3%	7.1%	84
Small Animal Practices	4.0%	5.8%	6.1%	7.9%	332
Feline Practices	3.7%	4.6%	6.0%	7.2%	16
Emergency/Critical Care Practices	3.2%	3.8%	4.6%	5.6%	26
Canada Total	4.4%	5.9%	6.1%	7.6%	27
Segmented by Region					
New England	3.9%	5.5%	5.5%	8.4%	23
Mid-Atlantic	3.9%	6.2%	5.8%	7.7%	36
South	4.0%	5.4%	5.8%	8.3%	50
Great Lakes	4.1%	5.7%	6.1%	7.1%	77
Plains	4.0%	5.5%	5.5%	6.6%	30
Northern Mountains	5.7%	9.5%	7.8%	9.5%	5
West	3.5%	4.8%	5.7%	7.7%	47
Pacific Northwest	3.6%	4.6%	4.9%	6.3%	22
Southwest	5.9%	7.6%	7.5%	9.3%	21
South Atlantic	3.7%	5.9%	6.1%	8.5%	46
Northern California	4.1%	5.7%	6.0%	6.6%	14
Southern California	3.2%	5.7%	5.8%	6.7%	17
Segmented by Number of Veterinarians					
1 Veterinarian	4.2%	6.6%	7.0%	9.8%	68
1.1–3 Veterinarians	4.6%	6.7%	6.7%	8.8%	186
3.1–5 Veterinarians	3.8%	5.4%	5.4%	7.1%	124
5+ Veterinarians	3.8%	5.0%	5.3%	6.2%	28
Segmented by Gross Income					
< $250,000 Gross Income	5.2%	8.9%	8.2%	11.1%	24
$250,000–$500,000 Gross Income	4.4%	6.4%	6.8%	8.5%	100
$500,000–$750,000 Gross Income	4.1%	6.3%	6.3%	8.2%	121
$750,000–$1,000,000 Gross Income	4.2%	5.8%	5.9%	7.6%	78
$1,000,000+ Gross Income	3.7%	5.0%	5.4%	7.1%	82
Segmented by Cost-of-Living Indices					
Low Cost-of-Living States	4.0%	5.7%	6.1%	8.3%	124
Average Cost-of-Living States	3.9%	5.6%	5.9%	7.6%	153
High Cost-of-Living States	4.0%	5.7%	5.8%	7.5%	97

Rent/Lease of Facility Expense as a Percentage of Gross Income

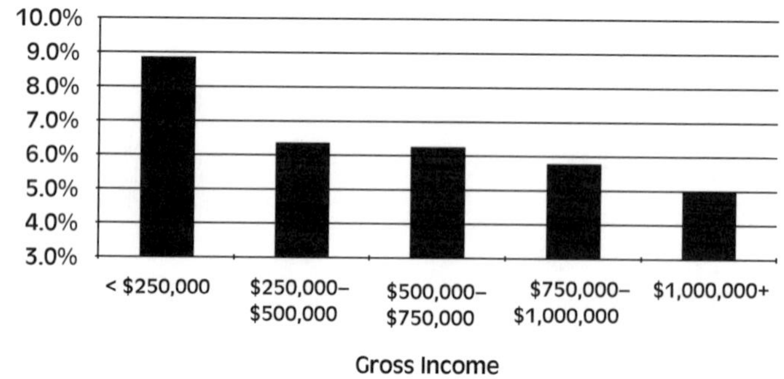

Rent/Lease of Facility Expense as a Percentage of Gross Income

Definition

Rent/lease of facility expense is not the same as mortgage payments. Except for the interest portion of the payment, mortgages do not show up anywhere on the income statement. Both the mortgage and the cash used to pay the mortgage are balance sheet accounts and do not affect the income statement. Rent/lease of facility, on the other hand, is an expense and does show up on the income statement.

If you pay rent to an unrelated party, you cannot do much to control this expense other than renegotiate your lease when it comes due or move to a different location.

Newer practices tend to show rent/lease of facility expense as much higher than the median because they are not yet producing income per veterinarian at the median level. As gross income increases, rent/lease of facility as a percentage of gross income should decrease to be more in line with the median.

If you pay rent to yourself because you own the property outside of the business, you know that rent is a tricky issue. You can manipulate it to be almost anything you want it to be, which means anything from 0% to 10% or more of gross income. The amount you pay yourself as rent is a decision you should make based upon carefully planned tax strategies that your CPA or tax attorney have created or reviewed.

If you own the property outside of the business and you do not pay yourself rent, you should consult with your accountant or tax attorney. Rent represents a fair return on your property investment. You may be missing an opportunity to reduce your tax liability by compensating yourself with rent in place of draw or salary. In addition, when you sell the practice, you may be unpleasantly surprised by the negative effect the absence of rent has on your practice's value. If you do not pay yourself rent, fixed expenses are artificially deflated and net income is artificially inflated. The person who values your practice, you can be sure, will take this into consideration.

In some areas, such as Hawaii, rent/lease of facility costs are extremely high. ATCs should be proportionately high to sustain the cost of occupancy.

Significant Findings

The U.S. median is 5.7%. Most regions are close to this number, except the Southwest and the Northern Mountains regions.

The data show that as a practice grows, in terms of gross income or in terms of the number of veterinarians, rent/lease of facility expense decreases as a percentage of gross income. In many cases, the practice's gross income grows more quickly than the does the cost of occupancy. This means rent expense as a percentage of gross income should decrease over time.

TOTAL EXPENSES AS A PERCENTAGE OF GROSS INCOME

General Overview	25th Percentile	Median	Average	75th Percentile	Number of Responses
U.S. Total (Mixed and Small)	66.0%	75.1%	74.9%	83.6%	453
Mixed Practices	67.4%	76.0%	75.0%	82.6%	84
Small Animal Practices	65.1%	74.9%	75.0%	84.0%	377
Feline Practices	65.3%	75.9%	78.0%	89.5%	15
Emergency/Critical Care Practices	71.6%	80.6%	81.2%	93.1%	26
Canada Total	63.4%	73.0%	73.5%	83.0%	40
Segmented by Region					
New England	71.6%	81.3%	80.2%	89.6%	24
Mid-Atlantic	63.7%	74.8%	73.7%	83.4%	49
South	64.7%	74.7%	73.0%	80.6%	63
Great Lakes	67.2%	75.4%	75.9%	83.0%	92
Plains	67.3%	74.6%	73.2%	81.6%	37
Northern Mountains	67.4%	80.0%	77.6%	81.5%	5
West	62.0%	71.5%	72.4%	82.1%	47
Pacific Northwest	66.8%	68.5%	71.5%	75.5%	16
Southwest	67.8%	82.4%	78.9%	87.8%	23
South Atlantic	67.3%	74.6%	74.1%	82.6%	45
Northern California	64.0%	74.4%	74.8%	85.9%	18
Southern California	70.8%	74.5%	75.7%	81.4%	19
Segmented by Number of Veterinarians					
1 Veterinarian	62.9%	73.2%	72.6%	81.6%	78
1.1–3 Veterinarians	65.4%	74.8%	74.0%	82.0%	218
3.1–5 Veterinarians	67.9%	75.4%	76.3%	84.7%	129
5+ Veterinarians	64.0%	75.1%	75.2%	85.8%	28
Segmented by Gross Income					
< $250,000 Gross Income	62.9%	74.7%	76.2%	88.3%	30
$250,000–$500,000 Gross Income	63.7%	75.0%	74.0%	82.7%	120
$500,000–$750,000 Gross Income	64.9%	73.9%	73.9%	81.5%	130
$750,000–$1,000,000 Gross Income	67.2%	74.2%	73.9%	82.1%	82
$1,000,000+ Gross Income	67.3%	75.4%	76.5%	85.5%	88
Segmented by Cost-of-Living Indices					
Low Cost-of-Living States	65.4%	74.4%	73.4%	81.5%	147
Average Cost-of-Living States	65.1%	75.1%	74.7%	83.4%	169
High Cost-of-Living States	68.1%	74.5%	76.2%	85.5%	104

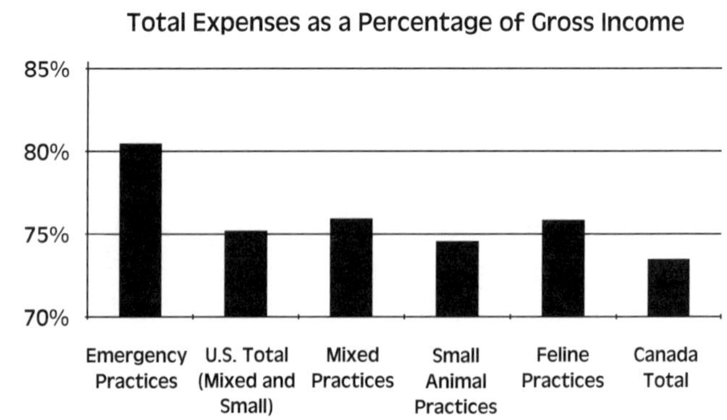

Total Expenses as a Percentage of Gross Income

Definition

Total expenses are all expenses except owner compensation. Expenses do not include payments on loans or other items on your balance sheet.

If your total expense figure is 2 or more percentage points above the median, you need to look further into specific expenses. Investigate which individual expense line items are higher than the medians.

If you are not producing enough income in your practice, your expenses may look too high as a percentage of gross income. For example, rent/lease of facility is a fixed expense regardless of how much revenue you generate. When you are not producing enough income, rent/lease of facility looks too high as a percentage of that income. Therefore, it may look as if you are spending too much money, but in fact you are not producing enough income (refer to the "Income per Veterinarian" section on page 25).

Significant Findings

The U.S. median for total expenses as a percentage of gross income is 75.1%. Two regions are significantly below this median (Pacific Northwest and West) and three regions are above it (Northern Mountains, New England, and Southwest).

The Pacific Northwest and West regions, which have the lowest median total expense percentage nationally, appear at the top of the net income before owner compensation scale (see page 50). Therefore, even though practices in the Pacific Northwest and West regions are not the top-grossing regions nationally, they realize the highest profit margins due to their low operating expense percentage.

There are no significant patterns in the total expense percentages in practices of different sizes.

NET INCOME BEFORE OWNER COMPENSATION AS A PERCENTAGE OF GROSS INCOME

General Overview	25th Percentile	Median	Average	75th Percentile	Number of Responses
U.S. Total (Mixed and Small)	16.4%	24.9%	25.1%	34.0%	453
Mixed Practices	17.4%	24.0%	25.0%	32.6%	84
Small Animal Practices	16.0%	25.1%	25.1%	34.9%	377
Feline Practices	10.5%	24.2%	22.0%	34.7%	15
Emergency/Critical Care Practices	6.9%	19.4%	18.8%	28.4%	26
Canada Total	17.0%	27.0%	26.5%	36.6%	40
Segmented by Region					
New England	10.4%	18.7%	19.8%	28.4%	31
Mid-Atlantic	16.7%	25.2%	26.3%	36.3%	49
South	19.4%	25.3%	27.0%	35.3%	63
Great Lakes	17.0%	24.6%	24.1%	32.8%	92
Plains	18.4%	25.4%	26.8%	32.7%	37
Northern Mountains	18.5%	20.0%	22.4%	32.6%	5
West	17.9%	28.5%	27.7%	38.1%	47
Pacific Northwest	24.5%	31.5%	28.5%	33.2%	16
Southwest	12.2%	17.6%	21.1%	32.2%	23
South Atlantic	17.4%	25.5%	25.9%	32.7%	45
Northern California	14.1%	25.6%	25.2%	36.0%	18
Southern California	18.6%	25.5%	24.3%	29.2%	19
Segmented by Number of Veterinarians					
1 Veterinarian	18.4%	26.8%	27.4%	37.1%	78
1.1–3 Veterinarians	18.0%	25.2%	26.1%	34.6%	218
3.1–5 Veterinarians	15.3%	24.6%	23.8%	32.1%	129
5+ Veterinarians	14.2%	24.9%	24.8%	36.0%	28
Segmented by Gross Income					
< $250,000 Gross Income	11.7%	25.3%	23.8%	37.1%	30
$250,000–$500,000 Gross Income	17.3%	25.0%	26.1%	36.3%	120
$500,000–$750,000 Gross Income	18.5%	26.1%	26.2%	35.1%	130
$750,000–$1,000,000 Gross Income	17.9%	25.8%	26.1%	32.8%	82
$1,000,000+ Gross Income	14.5%	24.6%	23.5%	32.7%	88
Segmented by Cost-of-Living Indices					
Low Cost-of-Living States	18.5%	25.6%	26.6%	34.6%	147
Average Cost-of-Living States	16.7%	24.9%	25.3%	34.9%	169
High Cost-of-Living States	14.5%	25.5%	23.8%	31.9%	104

Net Income Before Owner Compensation as a Percentage of Gross Income

Definition

Net income before owner compensation is the amount left over for a practice's owners after all expenses have been paid (except salary/ draw paid to owners). Obviously, the more owners you have, the more you must split up that available pool of money.

Significant Findings

The U.S. median net income before owner compensation as a percentage of gross income is 24.9%. In essence, this number is equal to 100% minus the total expense percentage in the previous section.

If a practice is to remain in business, it must be profitable. Even if your practice's gross income is not the highest, you still may be earning more money than practices with higher gross incomes because you are maintaining a higher profit margin. The example below illustrates that a practice can have a higher gross income figure but actually earn less than a practice with lower gross income.

Compare two regions: West and Southwest. Practices in the West region had a median 1997 gross income of $545,113 (see page 11) and netted 28.5% or $155,357; those in the Southwest region had a median 1997 gross income of $860,000 (see page 11) and netted 17.6% or $151,446. Practices in the Southwest region actually earned 57.8% ($860,000 versus $545,113) more in gross income than did those in the West region, but they had a net income of 2.6% less ($155,357 versus $151,446).

TOTAL SALARIES/DRAW PAID TO OWNERS AS A PERCENTAGE OF GROSS INCOME

General Overview	25th Percentile	Median	Average	75th Percentile	Number of Responses
U.S. Total (Mixed and Small)	11.8%	17.7%	18.7%	24.7%	540
Mixed Practices	11.8%	18.2%	19.1%	25.4%	114
Small Animal Practices	11.7%	17.6%	18.6%	24.2%	434
Feline Practices	9.1%	11.7%	15.9%	20.3%	16
Emergency/Critical Care Practices	3.2%	12.9%	13.2%	19.2%	25
Canada Total	14.6%	20.0%	20.1%	25.1%	42
Segmented by Region					
New England	9.6%	16.7%	17.2%	26.2%	29
Mid-Atlantic	12.9%	21.2%	19.8%	25.0%	50
South	11.6%	20.3%	20.3%	28.1%	69
Great Lakes	12.9%	18.5%	19.9%	27.2%	110
Plains	15.6%	19.5%	20.9%	26.6%	44
Northern Mountains	10.7%	10.7%	16.3%	20.1%	6
West	13.0%	17.7%	18.4%	22.9%	57
Pacific Northwest	5.4%	11.5%	14.1%	22.0%	27
Southwest	9.1%	15.4%	17.7%	24.8%	26
South Atlantic	10.3%	17.7%	17.9%	21.6%	55
Northern California	13.1%	17.8%	19.7%	25.1%	27
Southern California	9.5%	17.2%	16.4%	22.8%	20
Segmented by Number of Veterinarians					
1 Veterinarian	18.4%	26.8%	27.4%	37.1%	78
1.1–3 Veterinarians	12.1%	18.0%	19.0%	25.2%	260
3.1–5 Veterinarians	9.9%	16.7%	17.8%	24.2%	154
5+ Veterinarians	12.6%	17.9%	18.1%	23.0%	30
Segmented by Gross Income					
< $250,000 Gross Income	12.4%	20.0%	21.4%	29.5%	36
$250,000–$500,000 Gross Income	12.9%	19.5%	21.3%	29.0%	148
$500,000–$750,000 Gross Income	13.6%	19.4%	20.3%	25.9%	157
$750,000–$1,000,000 Gross Income	11.2%	16.8%	18.2%	23.2%	100
$1,000,000+ Gross Income	10.1%	16.0%	16.8%	22.8%	97
Segmented by Cost-of-Living Indices					
Low Cost-of-Living States	12.1%	19.5%	20.0%	27.6%	166
Average Cost-of-Living States	12.9%	17.7%	19.0%	24.7%	203
High Cost-of-Living States	9.9%	16.7%	17.6%	24.4%	133

Total Salaries/Draw Paid to Owners as a Percentage of Gross Income

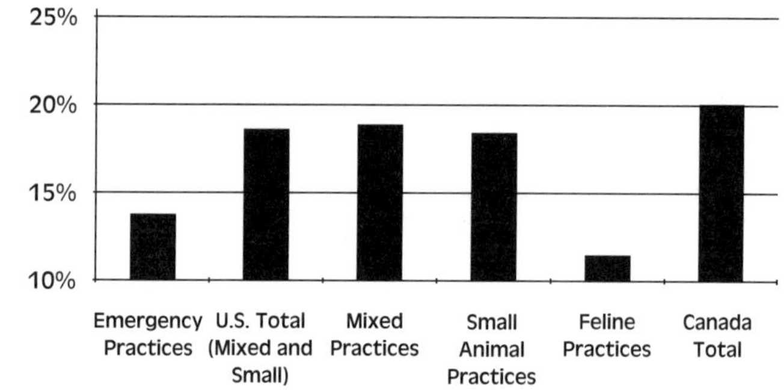

Total Salaries/Draw Paid to Owners as a Percentage of Gross Income

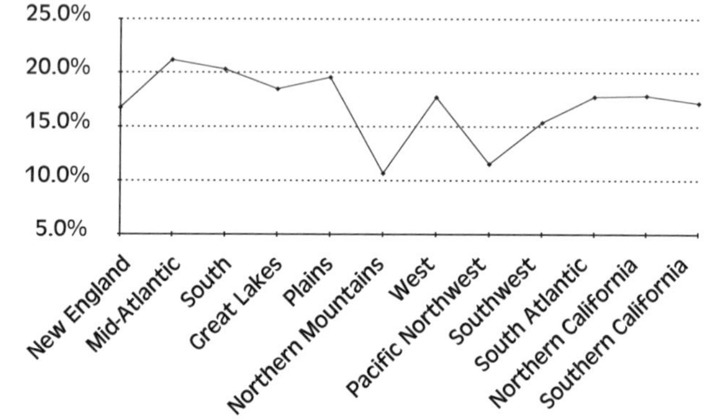

Total Salaries/Draw Paid to Owners as a Percentage of Gross Income

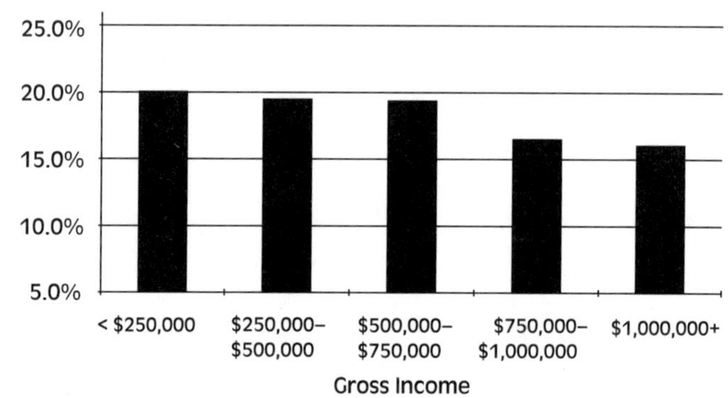

Total Salaries/Draw Paid to Owners as a Percentage of Gross Income

Definition

Total salaries/draw paid to owners is different from the net income before owner compensation discussed in the previous section because the owners will not receive every penny of the available pool of dollars. The number in this section is the amount actually paid out to the owners in the form of salaries/draw. The amount that is left remains in the practice, in the form of savings or to use for other purposes such as purchases of equipment or major building improvements.

Significant Findings

The majority of practices pay their owners a median of between 17% and 20% of gross income. The variance across the U.S. does not appear to be significant. However, when you convert the percentages to dollars, the differences are noticeable.

The conversion is simple: Multiply your region's median total salaries/draw paid to owners percentage by its median 1997 gross income number, which is a good approximation of your region's median dollar amount paid to its owners.

Two good examples of this calculation are the Pacific Northwest and Mid-Atlantic regions. Practices in the Pacific Northwest region have a median 1997 gross income of $646,157 (see page 11) and a total salaries/draw paid to owners percentage of 11.5%, which results in a total salaries/draw paid to owners of $74,501.

Conversely, those in the Mid-Atlantic region, with median 1997 gross income of $676,525 (see page 11) and a total salaries/draw paid to owners percentage of 21.2%, have a total salaries/draw paid to owners of $143,085, which is almost twice Pacific Northwest's figure. Some of this difference may be due to a higher cost of living. More details on owner compensation, as well as compensation and benefits for all staff members, are available in AAHA Press's *Compensation and Benefits: An In-depth Look*.

When analyzing the data as segmented by the number of veterinarians, it is apparent that owners of smaller practices draw more as a percentage of gross income than practices with more veterinarians. However, since their gross income is less than that of other practices, this does not necessarily equate to more compensation in terms of dollars. Smaller practices are probably forced to take most of their profit in compensation because the available pool of dollars is much smaller than in larger practices.

Assets and Liabilities

Balance Sheet Analysis in General

The balance sheet represents your financial position as it looks on any particular day. The balance sheet is divided into two sides, one showing your assets (what you own) and the other your liabilities (what you owe) and owner's equity. Both sides are always in balance.

The assets are separated into current and long-term. *Current assets* (including cash, accounts receivable, and inventory) are cash or those assets you intend to convert to cash within 1 year. *Long-term assets* (including land, buildings, equipment, furniture, and computers) are those assets that you don't intend to sell and that you regularly use to generate sales. The total of your current assets and your long-term assets equals your total assets for the practice. This figure will be equal to the sum of your liabilities and owner's equity.

Your liabilities are also divided into current and long-term. *Current liabilities* include all debts that are due within 1 year, including the portion of long-term debt (e.g., mortgage) that you must repay within 1 year.

Long-term liabilities are comprised of all debt associated with land or buildings as well as any deferred income taxes. Long-term liabilities correspond with your long-term assets (i.e., your long-term debt is debt you incurred to purchase your building, which is a long-term asset). The sum of the current liabilities and the long-term liabilities equals the total liabilities for your practice.

The final component on the balance sheet is your *owner's equity*, the practice's net worth. To arrive at this figure, subtract total liabilities from total assets. Part of the equity is expressed in the retained earnings figure, which shows a running total of profits that you reinvest in the practice. Equity also takes into account the initial investment of cash and other assets. Retained earnings will increase by the amount of profits earned less dividends or draw paid to the owners.

The relationship between assets, liabilities, and equity is an important gauge for your practice's financial health (see the "Quick Ratio" "Equity to Assets Ratio," and "Current Ratio" sections on pages 74 through 79).

CASH AND CASH EQUIVALENTS

General Overview	25th Percentile	Median	Average	75th Percentile	Number of Responses
U.S. Total (Mixed and Small)	$6,291	$16,549	$38,338	$40,204	544
Mixed Practices	$4,801	$10,998	$29,463	$35,638	118
Small Animal Practices	$6,948	$17,501	$39,958	$40,204	436
Feline Practices	$5,127	$8,412	$17,058	$25,157	18
Emergency/Critical Care Practices	$10,000	$48,000	$65,559	$91,436	27
Canada Total (in Canadian dollars)	$10,755	$28,864	$45,580	$61,977	41
Segmented by Region					
New England	$5,876	$12,160	$27,204	$31,417	30
Mid-Atlantic	$5,524	$26,614	$41,182	$59,055	53
South	$7,175	$15,500	$36,632	$42,588	75
Great Lakes	$5,959	$14,378	$33,522	$39,424	113
Plains	$3,808	$12,590	$27,429	$33,000	43
Northern Mountains	$7,600	$13,843	$16,999	$29,322	6
West	$6,000	$17,979	$27,981	$35,462	58
Pacific Northwest	$10,000	$35,000	$39,325	$70,000	25
Southwest	$9,566	$16,050	$41,279	$40,000	25
South Atlantic	$6,337	$13,346	$66,271	$31,472	52
Northern California	$13,468	$22,052	$71,494	$33,217	25
Southern California	$9,791	$14,500	$27,723	$33,000	19
Segmented by Number of Veterinarians					
1 Veterinarian	$2,500	$9,146	$25,926	$19,300	106
1.1–3 Veterinarians	$5,876	$17,200	$36,879	$42,000	255
3.1–5 Veterinarians	$10,000	$20,600	$43,301	$42,588	151
5+ Veterinarians	$11,688	$33,217	$64,767	$62,234	33
Segmented by Gross Income					
< $250,000 Gross Income	$1,100	$4,000	$16,102	$12,590	41
$250,000–$500,000 Gross Income	$5,651	$11,569	$19,892	$22,052	146
$500,000–$750,000 Gross Income	$6,500	$20,000	$45,512	$43,761	153
$750,000–$1,000,000 Gross Income	$10,000	$24,743	$43,985	$47,767	100
$1,000,000+ Gross Income	$10,836	$28,000	$58,607	$57,600	99
Segmented by Cost-of-Living Indices					
Low Cost-of-Living States	$7,310	$15,250	$34,623	$32,590	170
Average Cost-of-Living States	$5,524	$16,514	$41,371	$46,356	206
High Cost-of-Living States	$8,453	$19,000	$41,367	$40,000	129

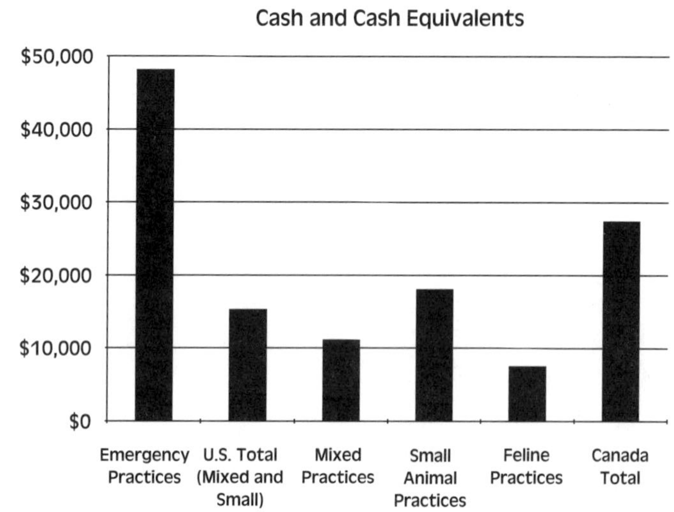

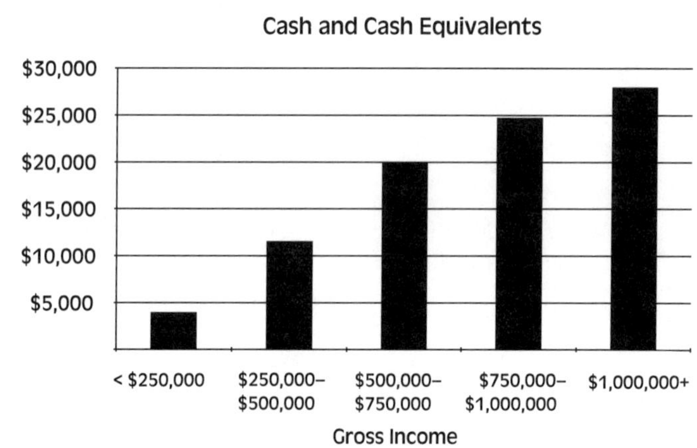

Cash and Cash Equivalents

Definition

Cash and cash equivalents consist of petty cash, cash on hand, checking accounts, savings accounts, and cash equivalents such as certificates of deposits. Make sure you have enough cash or investments that you can readily turn into cash to cover your current needs (see the "Current Ratio" and "Quick Ratio" sections on pages 74 through 77). You should be able to pay current liabilities as well as have a cushion to cover emergency expenses.

It is much easier to manage your practice's cash once you have created a system for keeping track of it. Such a system keeps you from getting in a bind when payroll or loan payments come due and prevents you from losing opportunities to earn interest on idle cash. This system is called a *cash budget;* it helps you plan for cash layouts well in advance so that you are never caught short.

When you evaluate your cash needs, consider how much higher or lower your gross income is than the 1997 median for your practice type. Remember: Everything is relative. A $1,000,000 practice needs more cash than a $250,000 practice.

If you have excess cash, invest it in interest-bearing short-term bonds, CDs, or money-market funds. Having a low cash flow probably indicates a much bigger problem. You should examine whether you are spending too much, not generating enough revenue, not budgeting properly, or a combination of all three.

Significant Findings

The U.S. median is $16,549, but the median varies a fair amount depending on region and practice size. In addition, the averages are quite different than the medians, which indicates that many practices have cash balances well above the median and are skewing the average upward.

There is a clear relationship between practice size, in terms of number of veterinarians and in terms of gross income, and the cash balance. As expected, the smaller practices have lower cash balances than larger practices.

You can also analyze cash as a percentage of gross income, which is an attempt to bring to a common level practices of different sizes. Here is data for selected practice types:

CASH AS A PERCENTAGE OF GROSS INCOME

	Median	Average
U.S. Total	2.7%	5.4%
Mixed Practices	1.8%	4.3%
Small Animal Practices	2.8%	5.7%
Feline Practices	2.2%	4.2%
Canada Total	4.6%	6.5%

As you can see, the medians and the averages for cash as a percentage of gross income are also quite disparate for the various types of practices. These figures indicate that practices are managing their cash in quite a wide variety of ways. When we evaluate cash as a percentage of gross income, there is no significant difference in these values either as the gross income increases or as the number of veterinarians increases.

Another way to tell if you have "enough" cash is through the quick ratio and current ratio (see pages 74 through 77). To manage cash wisely, your best tool for success is a cash budget. A cash budget is different from an operating budget in that a cash budget tracks cash in and cash out and the various sources and uses of that cash. An operating budget tracks income and expenses by category, and does not track certain types of transactions, such as purchases of equipment or payments on loans.

ACCOUNTS RECEIVABLE

General Overview	25th Percentile	Median	Average	75th Percentile	Number of Responses
U.S. Total (Mixed and Small)	$4,522	$10,619	$19,626	$23,212	539
Mixed Practices	$9,765	$21,863	$37,497	$41,000	115
Small Animal Practices	$4,000	$8,462	$14,469	$18,680	435
Feline Practices	$2,221	$3,358	$6,096	$6,400	18
Emergency/Critical Care Practices	$3,000	$10,476	$20,240	$30,276	25
Canada Total (in Canadian dollars)	$4,718	$9,900	$20,536	$27,642	42
Segmented by Region					
New England	$5,944	$13,262	$23,970	$25,641	31
Mid-Atlantic	$4,500	$10,000	$25,921	$24,929	54
South	$5,000	$10,169	$17,084	$21,500	70
Great Lakes	$4,178	$8,449	$17,957	$21,000	109
Plains	$3,335	$12,339	$25,676	$31,100	44
Northern Mountains	$13,785	$22,542	$30,739	$48,664	6
West	$4,500	$11,220	$14,503	$21,000	55
Pacific Northwest	$8,000	$14,598	$21,899	$37,405	25
Southwest	$10,000	$16,449	$26,554	$40,400	27
South Atlantic	$2,652	$8,690	$15,626	$16,000	54
Northern California	$8,462	$14,544	$18,722	$24,374	25
Southern California	$3,712	$9,348	$16,496	$25,352	20
Segmented by Number of Veterinarians					
1 Veterinarian	$1,950	$3,952	$6,484	$7,470	102
1.1–3 Veterinarians	$5,000	$9,679	$14,154	$17,000	254
3.1–5 Veterinarians	$10,000	$18,901	$28,314	$34,314	150
5+ Veterinarians	$31,004	$48,427	$70,564	$74,203	34
Segmented by Gross Income					
< $250,000 Gross Income	$1,100	$4,000	$16,102	$12,590	41
$250,000–$500,000 Gross Income	$2,700	$7,000	$9,835	$13,071	141
$500,000–$750,000 Gross Income	$5,000	$10,000	$15,705	$19,575	158
$750,000–$1,000,000 Gross Income	$7,261	$15,654	$22,822	$26,032	100
$1,000,000+ Gross Income	$13,593	$27,000	$43,521	$49,762	97
Segmented by Cost-of-Living Indices					
Low Cost-of-Living States	$3,535	$8,690	$17,790	$18,000	166
Average Cost-of-Living States	$5,245	$12,918	$21,783	$25,207	205
High Cost-of-Living States	$5,535	$12,000	$20,476	$25,641	131

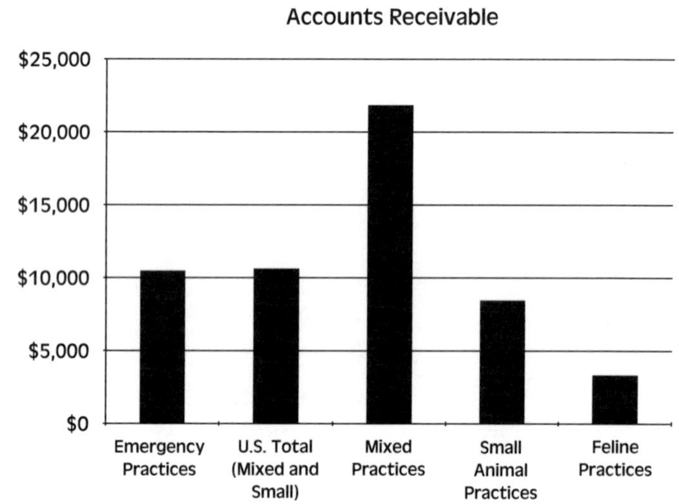

ACCOUNTS RECEIVABLE AS A PERCENTAGE OF GROSS INCOME

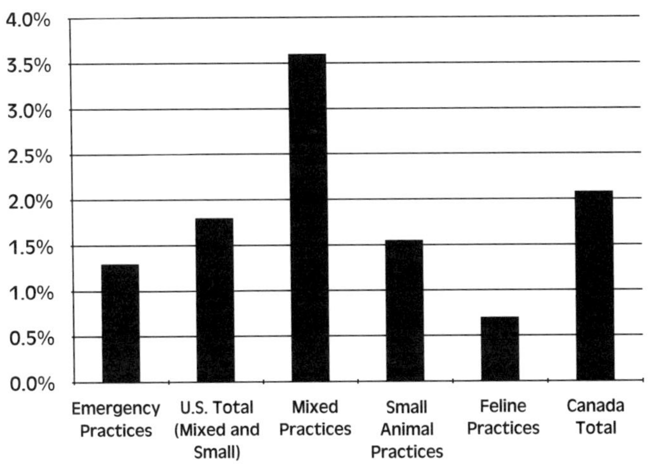

General Overview	25th Percentile	Median	Average	75th Percentile	Number of Responses
U.S. Total (Mixed and Small)	0.9%	1.8%	2.3%	3.1%	523
Mixed Practices	2.0%	3.6%	4.1%	5.7%	105
Small Animal Practices	0.8%	1.6%	1.9%	2.5%	429
Feline Practices	0.6%	0.7%	1.5%	2.1%	18
Emergency/Critical Care Practices	0.6%	1.3%	1.6%	2.1%	25
Canada Total	1.1%	2.1%	2.5%	3.3%	41
Segmented by Region					
New England	1.1%	2.0%	2.3%	3.8%	29
Mid-Atlantic	0.7%	1.5%	1.9%	2.7%	52
South	0.9%	1.8%	2.6%	3.6%	68
Great Lakes	0.8%	1.6%	2.3%	3.4%	106
Plains	1.1%	2.7%	3.4%	5.1%	43
Northern Mountains	4.8%	6.3%	5.6%	6.4%	6
West	1.1%	2.0%	2.2%	2.9%	53
Pacific Northwest	1.0%	1.9%	2.8%	4.6%	24
Southwest	1.4%	2.1%	2.7%	2.9%	25
South Atlantic	0.7%	1.3%	1.8%	2.3%	53
Northern California	1.1%	1.8%	2.2%	2.9%	25
Southern California	0.8%	1.3%	2.0%	2.9%	20
Segmented by Number of Veterinarians					
1 Veterinarian	0.7%	1.1%	1.9%	2.7%	99
1.1–3 Veterinarians	0.8%	1.7%	2.1%	2.9%	248
3.1–5 Veterinarians	0.9%	1.8%	2.5%	3.5%	145
5+ Veterinarians	1.8%	2.3%	2.9%	3.9%	31
Segmented by Gross Income					
< $250,000 Gross Income	0.6%	1.7%	2.5%	3.1%	38
$250,000–$500,000 Gross Income	0.7%	1.8%	2.3%	3.1%	136
$500,000–$750,000 Gross Income	0.8%	1.6%	2.2%	3.2%	155
$750,000–$1,000,000 Gross Income	0.8%	1.8%	2.5%	3.1%	98
$1,000,000+ Gross Income	1.1%	2.0%	2.4%	3.1%	93
Segmented by Cost-of-Living Indices					
Low Cost-of-Living States	0.8%	1.8%	2.5%	3.4%	161
Average Cost-of-Living States	1.0%	1.9%	2.4%	3.1%	198
High Cost-of-Living States	0.9%	1.8%	2.3%	3.1%	127

Accounts Receivable as a Percentage of Gross Income

Definition

Accounts receivable is a bone of contention for many practice owners and managers. Your practice philosophy will dictate whether you feel it is worth the price of lending money to clients in order to keep them as clients.

A few words of caution, though. Instead of earning interest, investing in equipment, or doing more advertising with the cash you *would* have had if the client had paid you for your services and products at the time of service, you are forced to find the money elsewhere. You may even find yourself *borrowing* money to lend money to your clients.

Reevaluate your credit policy periodically, both the myth and the reality. Is the staff enforcing the payment at the time of service rule only to have the veterinarian in the exam room say, "Oh, Mrs. Jones, I know you've been with us for 20 years, so pay whenever you can?" By keeping your accounts receivable in check, you can increase your operating efficiency from a cash flow standpoint.

Significant Findings

When you review the accounts receivable figures, you will notice that the medians for all regions are within the $8,000 to $16,500 range, with the U.S. median being $10,619. As expected, the accounts receivable dollar amount increases as practice size increases. Mixed practices have significantly higher accounts receivable than any of the other practice types, as these veterinarians generally do not collect for large-animal calls while on site.

By looking only at the dollar amount per region, you cannot get a true picture of how the accounts receivable relate to the gross income. A better method of examining accounts receivable management is to divide accounts receivable by gross income to show accounts receivable as a percentage of gross income.

The data shows that accounts receivable as a percentage of gross income increases as the practice size increases. One reason may be that over time, as practices grow, they have the flexibility to allow more and more clients to charge and allow clients to carry larger and larger balances.

INVENTORY

General Overview	25th Percentile	Median	Average	75th Percentile	Number of Responses
U.S. Total (Mixed and Small)	$12,533	$21,000	$30,442	$38,000	489
Mixed Practices	$15,000	$25,264	$33,854	$43,682	110
Small Animal Practices	$11,038	$20,000	$28,868	$35,000	390
Feline Practices	$5,512	$8,279	$11,123	$11,709	16
Emergency/Critical Care Practices	$5,000	$12,457	$20,593	$31,950	26
Canada Total (in Canadian dollars)	$15,000	$23,664	$29,722	$39,938	42
Segmented by Region					
New England	$12,305	$29,050	$52,727	$59,919	24
Mid-Atlantic	$14,365	$26,534	$31,470	$36,025	47
South	$13,000	$24,000	$28,909	$36,723	65
Great Lakes	$15,599	$24,000	$37,263	$49,346	103
Plains	$10,000	$24,569	$29,583	$47,536	43
Northern Mountains	$20,000	$32,965	$36,809	$42,628	5
West	$12,000	$17,425	$23,373	$24,000	55
Pacific Northwest	$8,332	$15,824	$19,832	$25,277	25
Southwest	$11,527	$25,250	$36,945	$53,187	21
South Atlantic	$9,200	$19,633	$23,667	$33,231	50
Northern California	$12,000	$17,059	$24,007	$28,259	23
Southern California	$16,000	$19,675	$26,498	$28,000	14
Segmented by Number of Veterinarians					
1 Veterinarian	$8,500	$15,000	$19,926	$24,000	95
1.1–3 Veterinarians	$12,000	$20,000	$27,297	$34,659	234
3.1–5 Veterinarians	$16,212	$28,600	$38,388	$49,750	135
5+ Veterinarians	$33,051	$58,201	$60,140	$83,377	26
Segmented by Gross Income					
< $250,000 Gross Income	$7,014	$12,650	$16,910	$20,098	38
$250,000–$500,000 Gross Income	$8,515	$15,742	$18,217	$24,000	138
$500,000–$750,000 Gross Income	$14,398	$22,347	$32,934	$39,000	139
$750,000–$1,000,000 Gross Income	$17,807	$30,116	$36,662	$47,945	92
$1,000,000+ Gross Income	$17,425	$38,164	$47,458	$62,072	78
Segmented by Cost-of-Living Indices					
Low Cost-of-Living States	$10,510	$20,000	$26,033	$35,000	161
Average Cost-of-Living States	$13,722	$23,114	$33,864	$43,919	187
High Cost-of-Living States	$12,624	$20,541	$31,993	$35,512	112

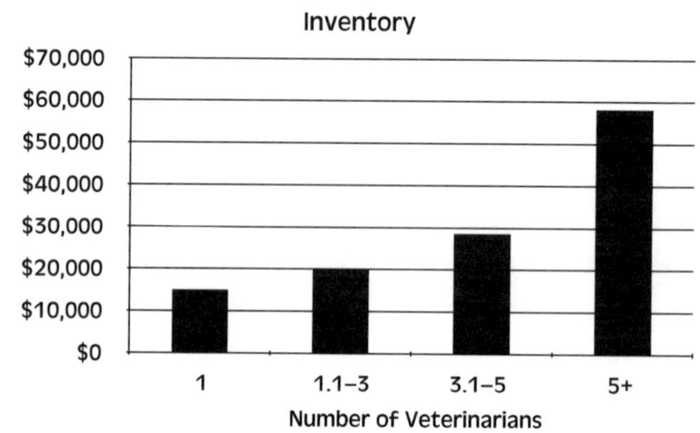

Inventory

Definition

Inventory includes drugs, ancillary services supplies, and medical supplies. The dollar amounts give you a good idea if you are way out of line when you consider how your practice's gross income compares to the U.S. median 1997 gross income.

Relate inventory levels to your annual drugs and medical supplies expense. Are both your inventory and drugs and medical supplies expense higher than the respective U.S. medians? (Inventory control is discussed further in the "Drugs and Medical Supplies Expense as a Percentage of Gross Income" section on page 35.)

Significant Findings

As expected, inventory increases as practice size increases. One-veterinarian practices carry a median of $15,000 and an average of $19,926 in inventory, while 5+ veterinarian practices carry a median of $58,201 and an average of $60,140 in inventory.

The U.S. median is $20,000 for small animal practices and $25,264 for mixed practices. Since drugs and medical supplies expense is higher for mixed practices (see page 34), and because they must carry more drugs to support the large animal side of the practice, it makes sense that their inventory is also higher.

You can also analyze inventory as a percentage of gross income, which is an attempt to bring to a common level practices of different sizes. Here is data for selected practice types:

INVENTORY AS A PERCENTAGE OF GROSS INCOME

	Median	Average
U.S. Total	3.4%	4.3%
Mixed Practices	4.2%	4.9%
Small Animal Practices	3.2%	4.1%
Feline Practices	2.2%	2.7%
Canada Total	3.8%	4.2%

The median U.S. practice carries 3.4% of gross income in inventory, while mixed practices carry 4.2% of their gross income in inventory. Our analysis showed no significant differences in inventory as a percentage of gross income as the practice size increases.

CURRENT ASSETS

General Overview	25th Percentile	Median	Average	75th Percentile	Number of Responses
U.S. Total (Mixed and Small)	$43,111	$80,521	$117,422	$143,393	509
Mixed Practices	$49,115	$91,742	$140,308	$183,700	109
Small Animal Practices	$39,112	$76,534	$108,184	$136,671	408
Feline Practices	$24,260	$35,736	$50,376	$72,452	16
Emergency/Critical Care Practices	$65,460	$124,500	$268,194	$320,916	28
Canada Total (in Canadian dollars)	$48,691	$86,324	$114,715	$148,645	41
Segmented by Region					
New England	$30,165	$69,904	$122,742	$171,768	26
Mid-Atlantic	$48,768	$89,738	$136,624	$160,000	46
South	$42,632	$82,185	$123,804	$139,781	70
Great Lakes	$51,228	$87,136	$104,508	$134,521	100
Plains	$41,570	$72,663	$115,870	$137,244	44
Northern Mountains	$36,405	$109,935	$102,764	$161,559	6
West	$37,963	$76,691	$109,222	$177,918	58
Pacific Northwest	$49,115	$81,898	$115,646	$149,353	25
Southwest	$32,625	$89,527	$109,583	$150,000	24
South Atlantic	$39,424	$56,947	$119,126	$135,165	50
Northern California	$49,461	$104,078	$146,856	$233,088	23
Southern California	$55,888	$97,092	$119,782	$145,959	19
Segmented by Number of Veterinarians					
1 Veterinarian	$25,000	$51,700	$108,668	$141,950	97
1.1–3 Veterinarians	$36,841	$76,323	$107,976	$135,165	238
3.1–5 Veterinarians	$54,817	$92,971	$123,489	$149,676	144
5+ Veterinarians	$111,996	$202,296	$198,590	$239,061	31
Segmented by Gross Income					
< $250,000 Gross Income	$20,957	$40,125	$92,035	$142,716	38
$250,000–$500,000 Gross Income	$32,710	$55,827	$99,709	$115,900	133
$500,000–$750,000 Gross Income	$40,650	$78,462	$113,242	$130,000	150
$750,000–$1,000,000 Gross Income	$60,740	$93,283	$121,502	$149,353	93
$1,000,000+ Gross Income	$68,784	$118,000	$157,796	$223,202	91
Segmented by Cost-of-Living Indices					
Low Cost-of-Living States	$43,111	$76,012	$118,069	$144,487	163
Average Cost-of-Living States	$39,712	$86,910	$116,671	$141,560	195
High Cost-of-Living States	$49,115	$80,059	$122,033	$165,943	118

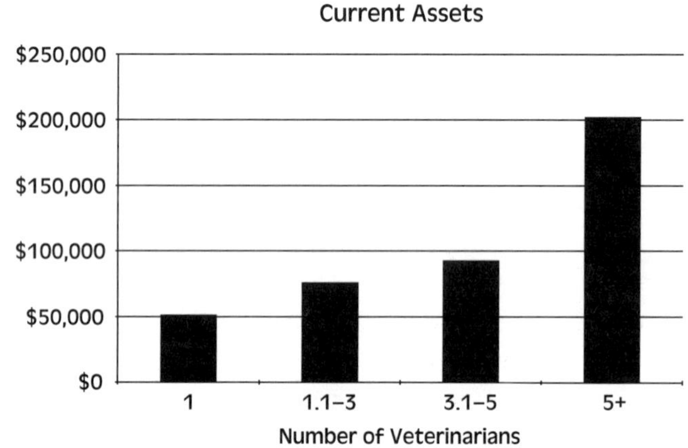

Current Assets

Definition

Current assets include cash and other assets that will be converted to cash within 1 year. For example, inventory is a current asset that will be converted to cash when it is sold. In addition, accounts receivable is a current asset because the debt will be collected within 1 year.

Significant Findings

Median current assets are generally in the range of $80,000, though they do vary by practice size.

To measure how the current assets relate to the current liabilities, see the "Current Ratio" and "Quick Ratio" sections on pages 74 and 76.

TOTAL ASSETS

General Overview	25th Percentile	Median	Average	75th Percentile	Number of Responses
U.S. Total (Mixed and Small)	$70,977	$146,313	$228,699	$283,600	529
Mixed Practices	$73,000	$155,647	$226,773	$300,000	114
Small Animal Practices	$67,787	$140,000	$224,866	$266,000	426
Feline Practices	$48,769	$97,222	$139,432	$139,012	19
Emergency/Critical Care Practices	$141,856	$221,692	$411,039	$567,043	28
Canada Total (in Canadian dollars)	$108,000	$207,873	$334,138	$446,485	42
Segmented by Region					
New England	$42,861	$88,704	$169,472	$317,754	25
Mid-Atlantic	$79,695	$180,916	$288,221	$316,478	49
South	$65,003	$155,570	$226,103	$299,738	70
Great Lakes	$83,195	$139,918	$217,212	$264,495	108
Plains	$76,823	$148,201	$210,429	$255,653	46
Northern Mountains	$50,800	$172,283	$146,800	$203,437	6
West	$57,177	$128,651	$204,829	$241,686	56
Pacific Northwest	$82,300	$149,631	$246,046	$346,000	25
Southwest	$60,113	$103,574	$222,264	$238,297	27
South Atlantic	$48,621	$133,277	$236,140	$267,793	53
Northern California	$78,750	$379,032	$365,704	$532,417	26
Southern California	$107,660	$214,088	$190,449	$246,519	20
Segmented by Number of Veterinarians					
1 Veterinarian	$40,991	$90,772	$171,895	$202,610	102
1.1–3 Veterinarians	$67,787	$150,000	$214,907	$267,763	245
3.1–5 Veterinarians	$96,617	$160,732	$257,074	$301,000	152
5+ Veterinarians	$179,566	$299,758	$465,842	$470,231	31
Segmented by Gross Income					
< $250,000 Gross Income	$42,250	$70,687	$182,888	$204,000	41
$250,000–$500,000 Gross Income	$54,422	$113,286	$177,708	$250,000	142
$500,000–$750,000 Gross Income	$65,799	$148,201	$227,757	$263,333	152
$750,000–$1,000,000 Gross Income	$90,406	$149,408	$229,235	$254,823	94
$1,000,000+ Gross Income	$133,277	$242,290	$332,856	$405,785	95
Segmented by Cost-of-Living Indices					
Low Cost-of-Living States	$64,354	$148,423	$215,950	$285,000	169
Average Cost-of-Living States	$80,589	$142,721	$232,655	$269,889	200
High Cost-of-Living States	$70,396	$175,000	$252,338	$349,209	127

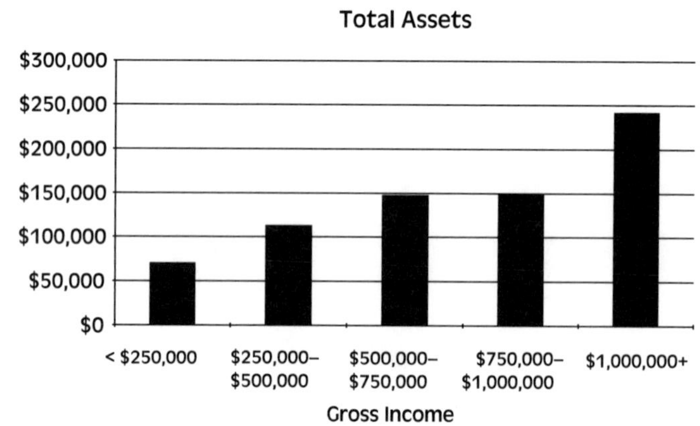

Total Assets

Definition

Total assets are current assets, such as cash and inventory, plus long-term assets, such as buildings and equipment.

Significant Findings

Total asset amounts vary widely across the country and by practice size. The U.S. median is $146,313.

To see how the total assets figure fits into your overall picture of financial health, see the "Equity to Asset Ratio" section on page 78.

CURRENT LIABILITIES

General Overview	25th Percentile	Median	Average	75th Percentile	Number of Responses
U.S. Total (Mixed and Small)	$8,596	$29,945	$53,146	$58,000	517
Mixed Practices	$10,100	$30,655	$58,632	$64,080	112
Small Animal Practices	$7,279	$29,711	$50,313	$55,600	414
Feline Practices	$2,700	$24,754	$45,663	$49,528	17
Emergency/Critical Care Practices	$5,000	$42,358	$123,094	$176,861	26
Canada Total (in Canadian dollars)	$24,308	$47,297	$90,712	$102,494	42
Segmented by Region					
New England	$12,198	$29,606	$75,766	$91,503	28
Mid-Atlantic	$5,864	$26,000	$59,171	$58,000	47
South	$9,380	$27,291	$44,345	$48,375	74
Great Lakes	$12,442	$38,530	$67,925	$82,374	106
Plains	$7,279	$21,215	$36,799	$49,623	42
Northern Mountains	$7,451	$17,751	$39,558	$56,928	6
West	$2,505	$12,500	$28,017	$33,361	53
Pacific Northwest	$13,739	$37,066	$53,559	$89,000	25
Southwest	$4,407	$23,887	$53,701	$43,291	26
South Atlantic	$7,000	$32,452	$55,385	$60,000	50
Northern California	$6,820	$37,294	$68,301	$70,265	22
Southern California	$10,850	$29,927	$62,978	$80,810	20
Segmented by Number of Veterinarians					
1 Veterinarian	$3,300	$13,124	$36,224	$37,837	98
1.1–3 Veterinarians	$7,279	$29,045	$48,791	$60,000	243
3.1–5 Veterinarians	$15,371	$40,290	$62,585	$65,950	146
5+ Veterinarians	$7,910	$35,411	$122,165	$128,801	32
Segmented by Gross Income					
< $250,000 Gross Income	$4,580	$13,430	$33,593	$40,000	40
$250,000–$500,000 Gross Income	$4,549	$13,150	$33,662	$39,893	136
$500,000–$750,000 Gross Income	$10,206	$32,784	$57,138	$68,000	150
$750,000–$1,000,000 Gross Income	$14,370	$39,817	$57,705	$66,534	92
$1,000,000+ Gross Income	$16,373	$43,080	$80,908	$93,526	94
Segmented by Cost-of-Living Indices					
Low Cost-of-Living States	$7,000	$26,200	$47,511	$52,000	165
Average Cost-of-Living States	$9,669	$27,338	$54,901	$57,168	192
High Cost-of-Living States	$9,750	$33,073	$57,601	$65,891	124

Current Liabilities

Definition

Current liabilities are bills, debts, or other obligations that the practice will pay within 1 year of the balance sheet date. For example, accounts payable are current liabilities that you need to pay off within 1 year (typically within 30 days). Your practice will use current assets (cash) to pay these current liabilities (bills).

Current liabilities also include the current portion of long-term debt, which is the amount of mortgages and other long-term debt that must be repaid within 1 year.

Significant Findings

Current liabilities do not vary as much as current assets do, with the median for most practices falling within the $25,000–$35,000 range.

There is no clear relationship between the number of veterinarians and the amount of current liabilities. In addition, for practices segmented by gross income, the only relationship seems to be a jump from around $13,000 in current liabilities in practices with up to $500,000 in gross income to more than $30,000 in current liabilities in practices with higher gross income. This is related to the fact that bigger practices have more long-term debt. The more long-term debt you have, the higher dollar amount of debt you must pay off each year.

To see how your current assets relate to your current liabilities, reference the "Current Ratio" and "Quick Ratio" sections on pages 74 and 76.

TOTAL LIABILITIES

General Overview	25th Percentile	Median	Average	75th Percentile	Number of Responses
U.S. Total (Mixed and Small)	$20,000	$59,777	$123,683	$154,009	535
Mixed Practices	$17,000	$55,000	$115,297	$129,739	119
Small Animal Practices	$21,603	$60,000	$124,151	$156,045	428
Feline Practices	$9,000	$72,256	$87,519	$135,906	19
Emergency/Critical Care Practices	$19,697	$103,532	$226,128	$354,000	27
Canada Total (in Canadian dollars)	$52,999	$135,619	$217,524	$277,560	41
Segmented by Region					
New England	$22,000	$58,392	$125,425	$203,492	27
Mid-Atlantic	$23,069	$74,893	$137,756	$183,919	48
South	$12,854	$57,272	$114,037	$127,469	72
Great Lakes	$34,196	$66,679	$129,818	$154,009	110
Plains	$14,000	$41,400	$90,317	$116,555	46
Northern Mountains	$9,383	$109,100	$76,652	$119,861	5
West	$10,736	$31,804	$91,092	$66,380	57
Pacific Northwest	$15,371	$59,968	$111,159	$140,000	26
Southwest	$23,575	$45,000	$151,344	$168,971	27
South Atlantic	$30,254	$72,350	$124,950	$193,000	51
Northern California	$25,264	$190,188	$251,818	$433,326	25
Southern California	$24,000	$127,072	$121,992	$219,743	21
Segmented by Number of Veterinarians					
1 Veterinarian	$7,400	$23,575	$59,354	$71,324	104
1.1–3 Veterinarians	$24,732	$61,279	$124,759	$158,560	248
3.1–5 Veterinarians	$36,311	$66,380	$149,364	$168,971	153
5+ Veterinarians	$85,622	$175,318	$255,331	$361,523	31
Segmented by Gross Income					
< $250,000 Gross Income	$8,000	$38,313	$74,882	$60,000	41
$250,000–$500,000 Gross Income	$10,000	$37,893	$87,588	$94,509	146
$500,000–$750,000 Gross Income	$27,179	$58,376	$112,486	$138,909	152
$750,000–$1,000,000 Gross Income	$33,784	$69,101	$118,595	$141,088	97
$1,000,000+ Gross Income	$54,481	$154,590	$229,240	$302,086	94
Segmented by Cost-of-Living Indices					
Low Cost-of-Living States	$15,442	$48,621	$106,543	$135,000	169
Average Cost-of-Living States	$23,575	$61,000	$119,645	$141,088	199
High Cost-of-Living States	$22,000	$81,442	$156,733	$255,749	130

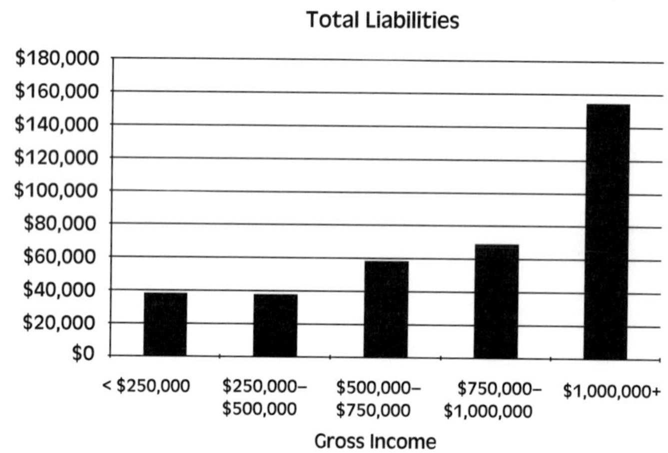

Total Liabilities

Definition

Total liabilities are current debt, such as accounts payable, plus long-term debt, such as mortgages.

Significant Findings

The total liabilities number varies widely based on practice size and region, with the U.S. median being $59,777.

The more gross income a practice has, the more debt it carries. The $1,000,000+ practices have about four times the debt as the practices in the <$250,000 category, so the amount of debt seems to increase at the same rate as the gross income.

To see how the liabilities relate to total assets, see the "Equity to Asset Ratio" section on page 78.

TOTAL EQUITY

General Overview	25th Percentile	Median	Average	75th Percentile	Number of Responses
U.S. Total (Mixed and Small)	$18,875	$72,984	$125,215	$167,744	439
Mixed Practices	$20,000	$82,239	$121,545	$182,888	102
Small Animal Practices	$16,765	$65,269	$122,417	$158,748	349
Feline Practices	$2,000	$18,715	$54,798	$66,472	18
Emergency/Critical Care Practices	$26,677	$107,740	$193,653	$293,953	27
Canada Total (in Canadian dollars)	$45,000	$119,165	$149,460	$258,028	34
Segmented by Region					
New England	$(12,412)	$25,424	$45,934	$82,239	20
Mid-Atlantic	$25,000	$109,400	$199,799	$215,301	37
South	$29,867	$102,245	$130,867	$205,554	59
Great Lakes	$17,701	$72,147	$112,010	$164,000	87
Plains	$29,846	$69,543	$129,981	$168,847	42
Northern Mountains	$18,569	$32,100	$64,508	$134,185	5
West	$25,905	$66,325	$128,953	$168,589	50
Pacific Northwest	$18,383	$82,000	$138,142	$148,690	24
Southwest	$13,564	$49,141	$91,184	$105,249	21
South Atlantic	$5,900	$61,202	$139,195	$167,000	41
Northern California	$60,014	$95,531	$150,613	$240,658	21
Southern California	$2,181	$58,822	$79,290	$145,224	16
Segmented by Number of Veterinarians					
1 Veterinarian	$12,960	$54,992	$127,629	$166,687	88
1.1–3 Veterinarians	$16,876	$62,949	$110,572	$155,000	198
3.1–5 Veterinarians	$26,529	$88,835	$127,569	$204,915	128
5+ Veterinarians	$62,979	$127,760	$250,993	$236,561	26
Segmented by Gross Income					
< $250,000 Gross Income	$16,178	$35,257	$125,448	$140,000	34
$250,000–$500,000 Gross Income	$23,233	$62,131	$99,915	$164,000	126
$500,000–$750,000 Gross Income	$18,062	$62,235	$138,480	$169,629	127
$750,000–$1,000,000 Gross Income	$25,208	$110,000	$151,354	$210,839	69
$1,000,000+ Gross Income	$48,030	$82,239	$125,471	$165,000	78
Segmented by Cost-of-Living Indices					
Low Cost-of-Living States	$18,493	$72,992	$123,625	$172,610	148
Average Cost-of-Living States	$25,905	$82,669	$139,650	$174,013	162
High Cost-of-Living States	$10,206	$63,628	$116,840	$166,373	103

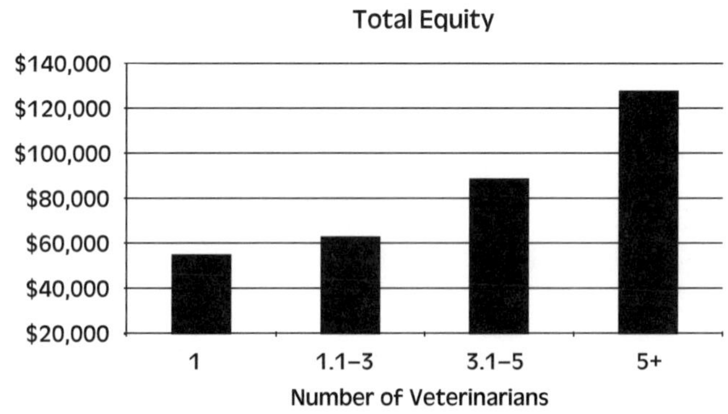

Total Equity

Definition

Total equity represents how much money the owners has invested in the practice, including retained earnings (net profit) and initial contributions of cash and equipment. Total equity is equal to total assets minus total liabilities. A practice with negative total equity has more debt than assets.

Draw or dividends paid to owners reduce the total equity figure. Salaries paid to owners in a corporation do not directly affect the total equity figure, but do have an effect through reduced net profit.

Significant Findings

Total equity varies quite a bit depending on the region. No obvious pattern links the dollar amount in total equity to practice size. The U.S. median total equity is $72,984 and the average is $125,215.

Total equity is an imperfect measure of which practices are "doing well" because the components of equity (capital invested in the practice and retained earnings) are not broken out. Practices in one region may be just as profitable as practices in another, but the owners are withdrawing profits from the practices instead of reinvesting them for future growth. This means that these practices' total equity is lower, but it does not necessarily mean they are less profitable.

To see how total equity fits into the bigger financial picture, see the "Equity to Asset Ratio" section on page 78.

Financial Ratios

These financial ratios are some of the same ratios that banks and appraisers will use to evaluate your practice's value or borrowing potential. These ratios do not tell you too much by themselves; rather, it is important to compare them over time to chart your progress.

Though it seems like you can use an infinite number of financial ratios to measure the health of your practice, we focus on three we consider most important: the current ratio, the quick ratio, and the equity to asset ratio.

CURRENT RATIO

General Overview	25th Percentile	Median	Average	75th Percentile	Number of Responses
U.S. Total (Mixed and Small)	0.65	1.14	2.42	2.41	447
Mixed Practices	0.71	1.78	2.83	3.12	94
Small Animal Practices	0.62	1.08	2.31	2.18	359
Feline Practices	0.55	0.65	0.79	0.76	12
Emergency/Critical Care Practices	1.05	1.41	2.19	2.16	25
Canada Total	0.23	0.56	1.23	1.36	40
Segmented by Region					
New England	0.66	1.09	2.14	2.21	23
Mid-Atlantic	0.52	1.84	3.43	3.81	39
South	0.80	1.10	2.61	2.30	64
Great Lakes	0.47	0.85	1.78	1.81	94
Plains	1.01	1.86	3.67	3.62	40
Northern Mountains	1.14	1.14	2.56	2.84	5
West	0.90	1.68	3.03	3.28	44
Pacific Northwest	0.37	1.32	1.85	2.24	21
Southwest	0.90	2.74	4.16	4.58	21
South Atlantic	0.71	1.37	2.48	3.12	44
Northern California	0.92	1.05	1.78	2.12	19
Southern California	0.49	0.89	1.76	1.71	18
Segmented by Number of Veterinarians					
1 Veterinarian	0.85	1.14	2.65	2.61	76
1.1–3 Veterinarians	0.69	1.16	2.29	2.24	211
3.1–5 Veterinarians	0.63	1.15	2.43	2.55	135
5+ Veterinarians	0.23	0.79	1.91	2.17	27
Segmented by Gross Income					
< $250,000 Gross Income	0.85	1.01	2.73	2.91	32
$250,000–$500,000 Gross Income	0.81	1.16	2.9	2.49	113
$500,000–$750,000 Gross Income	0.44	1.09	2.03	2.18	131
$750,000–$1,000,000 Gross Income	0.81	1.43	2.58	2.83	85
$1,000,000+ Gross Income	0.60	1.04	2.45	3.11	82
Segmented by Cost-of-Living Indices					
Low Cost-of-Living States	0.62	1.20	2.46	2.61	145
Average Cost-of-Living States	0.65	1.29	2.55	2.87	167
High Cost-of-Living States	0.60	1.05	2.15	1.81	104

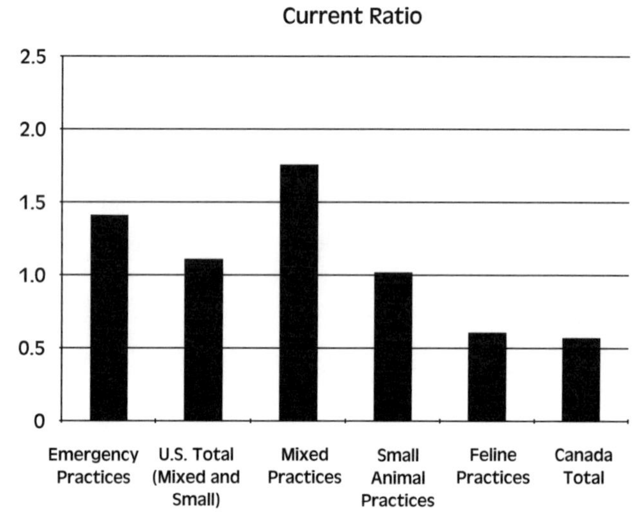

Current Ratio

Definition

The current ratio (current assets divided by current liabilities) measures your practice's overall liquidity and its ability to pay short-term debt. In other words, it indicates how well your practice can pay its bills each month. The current ratio is stated in terms of x:1, which means that for each dollar of current liabilities (bills), x dollars should be available in current assets (cash, accounts receivable, etc.) to cover those liabilities.

If the ratio is too low, your practice may not be sufficiently liquid to pay current liabilities or to take advantage of discounts for prompt payment. You probably need to keep more cash in the practice. If that cash is not available, you may have one of two problems: You do not generate enough revenue or you are not managing your cash very well. You need a cash budget to help you plan for future needs and how you will pay for them.

If the current ratio is too high, you may have excess cash, excess inventory, excess accounts receivable, or some of each. If your cash levels are above where they should be, make sure that you invest cash in short-term interest-bearing accounts. Having excess accounts receivable indicates a problem with your credit and/or collection policies. Having excess inventory means you need to take a closer look at ordering policies and procedures.

Significant Findings

The U.S. median current ratio is 1.14:1 and the average is 2.42:1. These figures mean that at least 50% of the practices have $1.14 in current assets for every $1.00 in current debt. Quite a few practices have significantly higher current ratios, which makes the average much higher than the median.

QUICK RATIO

General Overview	25th Percentile	Median	Average	75th Percentile	Number of Responses
U.S. Total (Mixed and Small)	0.34	0.83	1.81	1.86	404
Mixed Practices	0.27	0.83	2.06	2.15	89
Small Animal Practices	0.34	0.81	1.73	1.79	320
Feline Practices	0.44	0.58	0.61	0.58	11
Emergency/Critical Care Practices	0.94	1.38	2.13	2.72	23
Canada Total	0.15	0.15	0.91	1.02	40
Segmented by Region					
New England	0.40	0.45	1.04	0.91	18
Mid-Atlantic	0.19	1.33	2.58	2.86	35
South	0.45	1.07	2.3	1.77	55
Great Lakes	0.16	0.61	1.22	1.29	88
Plains	0.26	1.29	2.70	2.91	39
Northern Mountains	0.62	0.62	1.79	2.09	5
West	0.44	1.63	2.35	2.37	41
Pacific Northwest	0.10	0.74	1.53	2.12	20
Southwest	0.45	1.50	2.23	2.81	18
South Atlantic	0.35	0.89	1.98	2.71	42
Northern California	0.58	1.02	1.31	1.02	17
Southern California	0.19	0.80	1.49	1.48	14
Segmented by Number of Veterinarians					
1 Veterinarian	0.45	1.07	2.05	1.78	69
1.1–3 Veterinarians	0.27	0.83	1.73	1.89	194
3.1–5 Veterinarians	0.26	0.80	1.81	1.83	121
5+ Veterinarians	0.15	0.42	1.21	1.06	22
Segmented by Gross Income					
< $250,000 Gross Income	0.26	0.89	1.86	1.39	30
$250,000–$500,000 Gross Income	0.59	1.07	2.40	1.70	105
$500,000–$750,000 Gross Income	0.19	0.81	1.52	1.69	115
$750,000–$1,000,000 Gross Income	0.41	0.8	1.88	2.07	79
$1,000,000+ Gross Income	0.42	0.92	1.75	2.33	71
Segmented by Cost-of-Living Indices					
Low Cost-of-Living States	0.38	0.95	2.08	2.06	134
Average Cost-of-Living States	0.25	1.02	1.84	2.02	155
High Cost-of-Living States	0.34	0.75	1.51	1.69	90

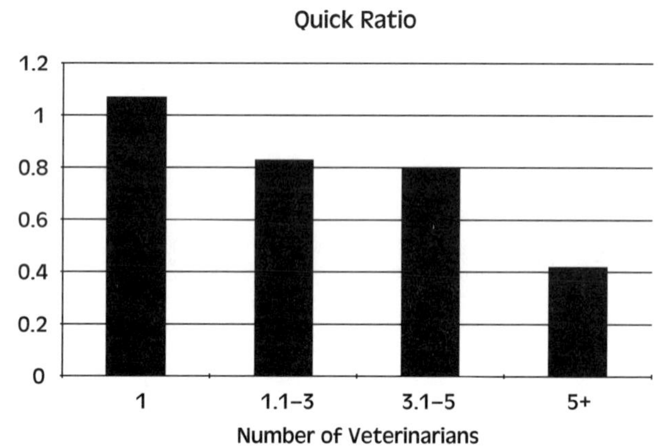

Quick Ratio

Definition

The quick ratio [(current assets – inventory) / current liabilities] is a measure of your practice's *immediate* (as opposed to overall) ability to pay current liabilities. This ratio will help you judge whether the practice is maintaining an efficient level of liquid assets to meet its current obligations.

The quick ratio measures how well your practice can meet its current obligations (bills) without having to depend on its inventory. Note that inventory is not included in this ratio because it may not be liquid or "quickly" sold. Therefore, it is not readily available for paying current liabilities or bills.

A practice with little cash available to pay current liabilities means additional risk for creditors.

Significant Findings

The U.S. median quick ratio is 0.83:1, which means that many practices would have only 83 cents in current assets for every dollar in current debts.

Practices with 5+ veterinarians have a median ratio of 0.42:1 compared to 1-veterinarian practices, which have a median quick ratio of 1.07:1.

To dig in a little deeper, let's more closely examine the practices in the West region, which have the highest median quick ratio. They have one of the lowest median dollar amounts of current assets (see page 64), so you do not have to have lots of current assets to have a high quick ratio. But they also have the lowest median dollar amount of current liabilities (see page 70). Their quick ratio is the highest of all the regions because they do not have an excessive amount sunk in inventory and because their current liabilities are lower than those of other practices.

EQUITY TO ASSET RATIO

General Overview	25th Percentile	Median	Average	75th Percentile	Number of Responses
U.S. Total (Mixed and Small)	0.12	0.56	0.47	0.84	520
Mixed Practices	0.17	0.62	0.49	0.79	115
Small Animal Practices	0.11	0.53	0.46	0.86	417
Feline Practices	0.06	0.63	0.37	0.64	19
Emergency/Critical Care Practices	0.07	0.29	0.27	0.51	24
Canada Total	0.18	0.35	0.36	0.69	40
Segmented by Region					
New England	0.00	0.17	0.27	0.62	24
Mid-Atlantic	0.16	0.74	0.54	0.96	49
South	0.00	0.56	0.49	0.85	68
Great Lakes	0.17	0.53	0.42	0.77	106
Plains	0.30	0.78	0.57	0.96	45
Northern Mountains	0.19	0.53	0.46	0.96	5
West	0.09	0.79	0.56	0.92	56
Pacific Northwest	0.23	0.70	0.54	0.95	25
Southwest	0.08	0.62	0.32	0.62	27
South Atlantic	0.41	0.69	0.47	0.80	51
Northern California	0.12	0.34	0.37	0.53	26
Southern California	0.00	0.39	0.33	0.65	20
Segmented by Number of Veterinarians					
1 Veterinarian	0.46	0.79	0.66	0.97	101
1.1–3 Veterinarians	0.02	0.51	0.42	0.81	239
3.1–5 Veterinarians	0.08	0.53	0.42	0.79	150
5+ Veterinarians	0.20	0.47	0.45	0.73	31
Segmented by Gross Income					
< $250,000 Gross Income	0.31	0.53	0.58	0.99	40
$250,000–$500,000 Gross Income	0.26	0.61	0.51	0.92	138
$500,000–$750,000 Gross Income	0.16	0.61	0.51	0.86	149
$750,000–$1,000,000 Gross Income	0.00	0.69	0.49	0.88	92
$1,000,000+ Gross Income	0.00	0.40	0.32	0.73	93
Segmented by Cost-of-Living Indices					
Low Cost-of-Living States	0.17	0.61	0.51	0.87	165
Average Cost-of-Living States	0.16	0.62	0.50	0.80	194
High Cost-of-Living States	0.01	0.34	0.39	0.89	126

Equity to Asset Ratio

Definition

The equity to asset ratio shows how much of the practice's assets the practice owns. For example, an equity to asset ratio of 0.50:1 means that the practice owners own half of the assets and outside creditors such as banks own the other half.

Newly built or newly purchased practices usually have equity to asset ratios much lower than the median because they have a relatively high amount of debt.

Significant Findings

Medians for the equity to asset ratio vary greatly among the various regions and sizes of practices. Somewhat surprisingly, 1-veterinarian practices have equity to asset ratios, which are much greater than those of other practices sizes. We would expect that more of the 1-veterinarian practices are newer, with higher debt loads. Perhaps those 1-veterinarian practices are more stable and not as newly formed as we thought in previous analyses. Also, the practices with more veterinarians may have relatively more debt because they have recently expanded, purchased new equipment, or moved into a new building.

Staff	25th Percentile	Median	Average	Your Data	75th Percentile	Number of Responses
Number of Full-time Equivalent Veterinarians	1.0	1.0	1.4	________	1.5	19
Number of Full-time Equivalent Nonveterinarian Staff	2.4	4.0	4.7	________	5.3	19
Number of Nonveterinarian Staff per Veterinarian	2.5	3.5	3.4	________	4.5	19
Number of Transactions per Veterinarian	3,199	3,988	4,100	________	4,814	17
Average Transaction Charge (ATC)	$61.47	$66.46	$72.77	________	$73.84	17
Income per Veterinarian	$245,227	$308,075	$299,793	________	$375,000	19
Income						
Laboratory Income as a Percentage of Gross Income	16.1%	17.5%	19.1%	________	24.6%	19
Radiology Income as a Percentage of Gross Income	1.8%	3.0%	3.0%	________	4.0%	19
Dentistry Income as a Percentage of Gross Income	2.8%	3.1%	3.6%	________	3.8%	19
Ancillary Services Income as a Percentage of Gross Income	10.7%	15.5%	16.5%	________	20.8%	19
Gross Income 1996	$240,000	$317,434	$371,800	________	$377,800	17
Gross Income 1997	$245,227	$375,000	$409,454	________	$427,600	19
Gross Income Growth Rate From 1996 to 1997	10.8%	14.8%	19.4%	________	18.6%	18
Expenses						
Drug and Medical Supply Expenses as a Percentage of Gross Income	7.2%	10.8%	11.6%	________	15.5%	17
Laboratory Expenses as a Percentage of Gross Income	2.5%	3.8%	3.8%	________	4.9%	18
Ancillary Services Expenses as a Percentage of Gross Income	5.6%	6.1%	7.4%	________	10.3%	15
Salary Expenses of Non-owner Veterinarians as a Percentage of Gross Income	3.3%	7.2%	6.8%	________	9.9%	11
Salary Expenses of Non-veterinarian Staff as a Percentage of Gross Income	17.2%	18.9%	20.7%	________	25.7%	17
Employee Benefit Program Expenses as a Percentage of Gross Income	0.9%	2.0%	2.3%	________	2.8%	14
Rent/Lease of Facility Expenses as a Percentage of Gross Income	3.7%	4.6%	6.0%	________	7.2%	16
Total Expenses as a Percentage of Gross Income	65.3%	75.9%	78.0%	________	89.5%	15
Net Income Before Owner Compensation as a Percentage of Gross Income	10.5%	24.2%	22.0%	________	34.7%	15
Total Salaries/Draw Paid to Owners as a Percentage of Gross Income	9.1%	11.7%	15.9%	________	20.3%	16
Assets and Liabilities						
Cash and Cash Equivalents	$5,127	$8,412	$17,058	________	$25,157	18
Accounts Receivable	$2,221	$3,358	$6,096	________	$6,400	18
Accounts Receivable as a Percentage of Gross Income	0.6%	0.7%	1.5%	________	2.1%	18
Inventory	$5,512	$8,279	$11,123	________	$11,709	16
Current Assets	$24,260	$35,736	$50,376	________	$72,452	16
Total Assets	$48,769	$97,222	$139,432	________	$139,012	19
Current Liabilities	$2,700	$24,754	$45,663	________	$49,528	17
Total Liabilities	$9,000	$72,256	$87,519	________	$135,906	19
Total Equity	$2,000	$18,715	$54,798	________	$66,472	18
Current Ratio	0.6	0.7	0.8	________	0.8	12
Quick Ratio	0.4	0.6	0.6	________	0.6	11
Equity to Asset Ratio	0.1	0.6	0.4	________	0.6	19

Feline Practice Analysis

Nineteen feline practices responded to this survey. For any survey, there are varying levels of confidence in the results, depending on the number of responses. Nineteen responses represent a confidence level of 90% (±19%. This means you can feel comfortable the results for this analysis pertain to 90% of feline practices with a margin of error of 19% for each data point.

Staff

The number of veterinarians in feline practices is generally smaller than in their nonspecies-specific small animal counterparts. Feline practices have a median of 1.0 veterinarian versus the U.S. median of 2.0 veterinarians. The 75th percentile for number of veterinarians in feline practices is only 1.5, which indicates that feline practices rarely have more than 2 veterinarians. This makes sense because feline practitioners have a limited market compared to other small animal practices.

Because the number of veterinarians is lower than in other kinds of practices, it follows that the number of full-time equivalent nonveterinarian staff is lower as well. Feline practices have a median of 4.0 and an average of 4.7 staff compared to the U.S. median of 6.0 and average of 7.6.

The number of nonveterinarian staff per veterinarian in feline practices (3.5) is higher than the U.S. median (3.0). One reason for this may be that feline practices use more nonveterinarian staff per veterinarian in order to provide a "high-touch" client service environment.

Income

Because feline practices have fewer veterinarians than other practices, you would expect their gross income to be lower as well. This is true if you compare the median 1997 gross income of $375,000 to the U.S. median of $622,541. However, look at the feline median gross income of $375,000 compared to the median for 1-veterinarian practices, which is $305,500. The feline practices compare very favorably. In addition, the feline practices' average 1997 gross income of $409,454 outperforms the average for 1-veterinarian practices of $322,328 by 27%.

The gross income growth rate from 1996 to 1997 was significantly higher for feline practices than for other practices. The median growth rate for feline practices was 14.8% versus an 8.0% growth rate for small animal practices in general. One-veterinarian practices experienced an even lower growth rate of 6.0%. The disparity in growth rates suggests that feline practices are filling a niche clients that agree is important.

Laboratory income made up a far larger percentage of gross income in feline practices than in other practices. The median laboratory income for feline practices was 17.5%, while the U.S. median for small animal practices was 12.6% and the median for 1-veterinarian practices was 11.4%. Note that in the 75th percentile, laboratory income accounts for almost 25% of feline practices' gross income. The 75th percentile for small animal practices is just over 15%.

Interestingly, radiology income showed a similar trend. While feline practices were close to the U.S. median of 2.9%, they were significantly above the 1-veterinarian median of 2.2%.

The median percentage of gross income derived from dentistry for feline practices (3.1%) was almost twice that of small animal practices (1.6%). These data suggest that feline practices are doing a much better job of educating clients about the importance of dentistry and marketing dentistry to clients.

For feline practices, median ancillary services income is 2 percentage points above that of other small animal practices, at 15.5% versus 13.5%. This could be because feline practices provide relatively more boarding services than other practices.

Productivity

The number of transactions per veterinarian for feline practices (3,988) is quite a bit lower than the U.S. median of 4,634, and much lower than that for 1-veterinarian practices, which have a median of 5,012. On the other hand, the feline practices' ATC of $66.46 is somewhat higher than the U.S. median of $59.76 and compares favorably to 1-veterinarian practices' median ATC of $53.26. Because feline practices' dentistry and laboratory incomes are so much higher than those for other practices, the high ATC is not surprising.

The combined effect of the higher ATC and the lower number of transactions per veterinarian is that the income per veterinarian for feline practices is about $29,000 more than U.S. median, at $308,075 versus $279,284.

Expenses

Feline practices are spending 4% less of their gross income than their small animal counterparts on drugs and medical supplies (see page 34). Obviously, concentrating on one species has its advantages when it comes to carrying drugs.

As you would expect, median laboratory expenses are much higher for feline practices (3.8%) than for other practices. The U.S. median for laboratory expenses is 2.5%. However, the true test for profitability is the laboratory markup percentage. Feline practices are marking up their laboratory services by 360%, whereas the median is about 350% (see page 36). Since their markup is about the same, increased fees cannot explain feline practices' higher percentage of laboratory income. Rather, feline practices must offer and recommend laboratory services much more frequently than other practices.

Ancillary services expenses are higher for feline practices than for others, but that is to be expected because they have higher ancillary services income (see page 38). The U.S. median markup on ancillary services is 195%, while feline practices have a 155% markup. This discrepancy may be because they are pricing their products and services lower than they could be, but it may also be because they have a very different mix of products and services than other practices.

The median for salary expenses of associate veterinarians for feline practices (7.2%) is lower than the U.S. median (8.4%). However, feline practices' associate veterinarian expense is much higher than that for 1-veterinarian practices (2.4%). This could be because feline practice owners spend relatively less time in the practice and hire more associate veterinarians than do small animal practice owners.

Feline practices spend a little less on nonveterinarian staff salaries than the U.S. median and slightly more than the median for 1-veterinarian practices. Their employee benefits program expenses seem to be about the same as those for other practices (see pages 42 and 44).

Feline practices had low median rent/lease of facility expenses of 4.6%. This number is well below the U.S. median of 5.7% and below the median of 6.6% for 1-veterinarian practices. One conclusion you could draw from this data is that feline practices need less square footage to operate than their 1-veterinarian small animal counterparts.

Since feline practices seem to be doing so well in terms of controlling expenses in a couple key areas, it is surprising that their total expenses percentage is almost 76%, as compared to the U.S. median of 75.1% and the median of 73.2% for 1-veterinarian practices.

But when you compare the major expenses to the medians, you can see why. Feline practices spend 1.1% less on rent/lease of facility expenses and 4% less on drugs expense. On the other hand, their laboratory expenses are 1.2% higher, their ancillary services expenses are 1.7% higher, and their associate veterinarians salary expense is almost 5% higher. The net difference is 3% of gross income, which equates to the 2.7% difference between the 75.9% in total expenses for feline practices and 73.2% for 1-veterinarian practices.

Owner Compensation

Because feline practices' total expenses are higher than the U.S. median, the net income before owner compensation is correspondingly lower than the U.S. median. Owners of feline practices are netting less, and they are also taking less out of their practices than other owners, especially compared to other 1-veterinarian practices.

The median for total salaries/draw paid to owners in feline practices is 11.7% and the average is 15.9%. Compare these figures to the U.S. median of 17.7%, a U.S. average of 18.7%, a 1-veterinarian median of 26.8%, and a 1-veterinarian average of 27.4%. This discrepancy may mean that feline owners retain more of their profits within the practice in order to grow the business (i.e., they invest in new assets to generate additional income).

Assets and Liabilities

The cash balance is relatively low in feline practices (see page 56), which may be because that cash is spent on acquiring new assets. If this were true, you would probably expect the feline practices' equity to asset ratio to be higher than it is. (See page 79 for an explanation of this ratio.)

In other words, if the feline practices were spending cash on equipment, the cash levels would be relatively low but the total assets would be relatively high and the total debt would be relatively low compared to the medians for 1-veterinarian practices. Since this is not the case, it may be that feline practices are spending their cash on new assets by expensing the maximum allowed per year by the Internal Revenue Service ($18,500 in 1998). This would explain the absence of assets on the balance sheet.

Accounts receivable are extremely low compared to the U.S. median, both in terms of dollars and as a percentage of gross income (see pages 58 and 59). Compared to 1-veterinarian practices, the dollar amount of accounts receivable for feline practices is a little lower, and the accounts receivable as a percentage of gross income is 0.7% compared to 1.1%.

Inventory is also low compared to the U.S. median and compared to the median for 1-veterinarian practices (see page 62). This difference is appropriate because feline practices have a lower drugs expense than small animal practices and 1-veterinarian practices.

Feline practices have relatively high levels of debt and low equity, which may be because they are fairly new practices. The current and quick ratios are poor, due to lots of current debt combined with low cash balances, low inventory balances, and low accounts receivable (see pages 56, 62, and 58). The only way to improve these ratios is to keep more cash in the practices, either by reducing owner compensation, by cutting expenses, or by generating more revenue.

Staff	25th Percentile	Median	Average	Your Data	75th Percentile	Number of Responses
Number of Full-time Equivalent Veterinarians	1.5	2.5	2.6	______	3.3	43
Number of Full-time Equivalent Nonveterinarian Staff	3.0	5.3	5.9	______	8.0	43
Number of Nonveterinarian Staff per Veterinarian	1.7	2.0	2.3	______	2.6	43
Number of Transactions per Veterinarian	3,239	4,042	4,217	______	4,497	35
Average Transaction Charge (ATC) (in Canadian dollars)	$56.47	$63.38	$65.01	______	$74.71	36
Income per Veterinarian (in Canadian dollars)	$224,876	$270,717	$276,547	______	$292,778	43
Income						
Laboratory Income as a Percentage of Gross Income	6.0%	7.7%	8.5%	______	10.5%	37
Radiology Income as a Percentage of Gross Income	1.8%	2.4%	2.8%	______	3.4%	40
Dentistry Income as a Percentage of Gross Income	1.3%	1.7%	2.2%	______	2.7%	38
Ancillary Services Income as a Percentage of Gross Income	7.6%	14.2%	15.7%	______	22.5%	38
Gross Income 1996 (in Canadian dollars)	$381,084	$612,807	$694,902	______	$938,794	40
Gross Income 1997 (in Canadian dollars)	$389,730	$627,717	$705,388	______	$950,632	43
Gross Income Growth Rate From 1996 to 1997	1.6%	5.2%	5.4%	______	9.2%	40
Expenses						
Drug and Medical Supply Expenses as a Percentage of Gross Income	10.5%	16.2%	16.7%	______	23.1%	40
Laboratory Expenses as a Percentage of Gross Income	1.4%	2.3%	2.3%	______	2.9%	38
Ancillary Services Expenses as a Percentage of Gross Income	4.1%	7.2%	7.4%	______	10.0%	25
Salary Expenses of Nonowner Veterinarians as a Percentage of Gross Income	4.5%	7.5%	7.5%	______	9.5%	33
Salary Expenses of Nonveterinarian Staff as a Percentage of Gross Income	16.9%	18.9%	19.8%	______	21.7%	32
Employee Benefit Program Expenses as a Percentage of Gross Income	0.7%	1.0%	1.6%	______	2.6%	28
Rent/Lease of Facility Expenses as a Percentage of Gross Income	4.4%	5.9%	6.1%	______	7.6%	27
Total Expenses as a Percentage of Gross Income	63.4%	73.0%	73.5%	______	83.0%	40
Net Income Before Owner Compensation as a Percentage of Gross Income	17.0%	27.0%	26.5%	______	36.6%	40
Total Salaries/Draw Paid to Owners as a Percentage of Gross Income	14.6%	20.0%	20.1%	______	25.2%	42
Assets and Liabilities						
Cash and Cash Equivalents (in Canadian dollars)	$10,755	$28,864	$45,580	______	$61,977	41
Accounts Receivable (in Canadian dollars)	$4,718	$9,900	$20,536	______	$27,642	42
Accounts Receivable as a Percentage of Gross Income	1.1%	2.1%	2.5%	______	3.3%	41
Inventory (in Canadian dollars)	$15,000	$23,664	$29,722	______	$39,938	42
Current Assets (in Canadian dollars)	$48,691	$86,324	$114,715	______	$148,645	41
Total Assets (in Canadian dollars)	$108,000	$207,873	$334,138	______	$446,485	42
Current Liabilities	$24,308	$47,297	$90,712	______	$102,494	42
Total Liabilities	$52,999	$135,619	$217,524	______	$277,560	41
Total Equity	$45,000	$119,165	$149,460	______	$258,028	34
Current Ratio	0.2	0.6	1.2	______	1.4	40
Quick Ratio	0.2	0.2	0.9	______	1.0	40
Equity to Asset Ratio	0.2	0.4	0.4	______	0.7	40

Canadian Practice Analysis

Forty-three practices in Canada responded to this survey. For any survey, there are varying levels of confidence in the results, depending on the number of responses. Forty-three responses represent a confidence level of 98% (±18%. This means you can feel comfortable the results for this analysis pertain to 98% of the practices in Canada with a margin of error of 18% for each data point.

Staff

Practices in Canada have more veterinarians than practices in the United States, with a median of 2.5 veterinarians and an average of 2.6, versus the U.S. figures of 2.0 and 2.4, respectively. However, practices in Canada have fewer nonveterinarian staff; the median number of staff is 5.3 compared to the U.S. median of 6.0, and the average is 5.9 compared to the U.S. average of 7.6.

As you would expect, these figures result in a lower number of staff per veterinarian. In fact, practices in Canada operate with a median of 1.0 fewer staff per veterinarian (2.0) than U.S. practices (3.0).

Income

The first thing you need to consider is that the dollar amounts listed for practices in Canada are stated in Canadian dollars, where the dollar amounts listed for U.S. practices are in U.S. dollars. At the time this was written, the exchange rate was $1 Canadian was equal to $0.67 U.S. In other words, a person could have exchanged $100 Canadian for $67 U.S. When the Canadian dollars are converted to their U.S. equivalents, we can better compare the practices in Canada to those in the United States.

When you convert the Canadian dollar amounts to U.S. dollars, practices in Canada are, overall, 50% smaller in terms of gross income than their U.S. counterparts. The median gross income in U.S. dollars in 1997 was $420,570 and the average was $472,576. Compare these to the U.S. numbers of $622,541 and $707,704, respectively. Of course, the comparison of gross income by itself is only one piece of the complete picture. Another important piece that allows you to compare practices of different sizes is the income per veterinarian (see the "Productivity" section).

The gross income growth rate from 1996 to 1997 was lower in Canadian practices than in U.S. practices. The median growth rate for practices in Canada was 5.2% versus a U.S. median growth rate of 7.5%. Both the Canadian and U.S. inflation rates were just over 1.5% in 1997, so the U.S. practices are growing relatively faster than their Canadian counterparts.

As a percentage of gross income, the Canadian median laboratory income was 7.7% versus the U.S. median of 11.9%. Even in the 75th percentile, laboratory income accounted for only 10.5% of Canadian practices' gross income. You might expect this to negatively affect the ATC, and we do see that practices in Canada have significantly lower ATCs than U.S. practices (see the "Productivity" section below). The median markup on laboratory services in Canada is 235%, which is low compared to the U.S. median of 376% (see page 36). A low markup also contributes to a lower ATC.

Radiology income as a percentage of gross income is also low compared to that of practices in the United States. The median for practices in Canada is 2.4%, and the U.S. median is 2.9%.

The median and average percentages of gross income derived from dentistry in Canadian practices are slightly higher than the U.S. figures, at 1.7% and 2.2% versus 1.5% and 1.9%.

Ancillary services income is about 1 percentage point above that for U.S. practices, at a median of 14.2% versus 13.3%. The median markup on ancillary services in the United States is about 200%. The markup in practices in Canada, which is only 97%, compares unfavorably to that of U.S. practices (see page 38).

Productivity

The median number of transactions per veterinarian in Canada (4,042) is quite a bit lower than the U.S. median of 4,634, and significantly lower than that for 1.1–3 veterinarian practices, which have 4,806 transactions per veterinarian. *Note: This may be a major reason why practices in Canada require fewer nonveterinarian staff per veterinarian than those in the United States.*

Once you convert the Canadian practices' ATC to U.S. dollars, you see that the median Canadian ATC of $42.46 is also much lower than the U.S. median of $59.76. In addition, it compares unfavorably to the median ATC of $58.41 for practices with 1.1–3 veterinarians. The combined effect of the lower ATC and the lower number of transactions per veterinarian is that the income per veterinarian in Canada is about $100,000 U.S. less than U.S. median, at $181,380 versus $279,284.

Expenses

Practices in Canada spend about one-half of a percentage point more on drugs and medical supplies as a percentage of gross income than U.S. practices. The median is 16.2% compared to the U.S. median of 15.6%.

Laboratory expense as a percentage of gross income is about the same in the United States (2.5%) as in Canada (2.3%), but as mentioned earlier, the markup on laboratory services is much lower.

Ancillary services expense is much higher for practices in Canada, and again their markup is much lower than in the United States. Canadian practices may be pricing their products and services lower than they could be or they may have a very different mix of products and services than U.S. practices.

Practices in Canada are about one percentage point lower than the U.S. median for associate veterinarians salary expenses as a percentage of gross income. However, the median Canadian expense of 7.5% is about the same as those for U.S. practices with 1.1–3 veterinarians at a median of 7.2%.

Canadian practices spend a little less on nonveterinarian staff salaries as a percentage of gross income than the U.S. median, which is because their staff per veterinarian ratio is lower than in the United States. In fact, since they operate with 1 fewer full-time equivalent nonveterinarian staff than U.S. practices, you might think that their staff salaries expenses would be much lower. However, as we saw in the "Productivity" section, the income per veterinarian is much lower for practices in Canada, which makes the staff salaries expense look much higher as a percentage of gross income.

The amount spent on employee benefits (a median of 1.0% of gross income in Canada) is lower than in U.S. practices, which spend 2.0%. Since practices in Canada do not have to pay for health insurance, we would expect their employee benefits program expenses to be lower than in the United States.

Rent/lease of facility expenses as a percentage of gross income in Canada (a median of 5.9%) seems to be right in line with those in the United States (a median of 5.7%).

The total expenses figure for practices in Canada is a median of 73.0% compared to the U.S. median of 75.1% and a median of 74.8% for U.S. practices with 1.1–3 veterinarians. This comes as a bit of a surprise since practices in Canada have to pay so much more in taxes than do practices in the United States. Perhaps they save in other areas for which we did not collect data.

Owner Compensation

Because total expenses of Canadian practices are slightly lower than the U.S. median, their net income before owner compensation is correspondingly higher than the U.S. median. Practice owners in Canada net more in terms of percentage of gross income, but they have less available to take out of their practices than do U.S. practice owners in terms of U.S. dollars. The median pool of available dollars (net income before owner compensation) is $113,554 in Canadian practices and $155,013 in U.S. practices.

Note: Derived from the following equation: (gross income) × (net income before owner compensation as a percentage of gross income)

The median for total salaries/draw paid to owners as a percentage of gross income in Canadian practices is 20.0% compared to a U.S. median of 17.7%. This discrepancy may mean that Canadian practice owners do not retain as much of their profits in the practice to grow the business. However, this is understandable when you see that 20.0% of the 1997 median gross income for Canadian practices is equal to $84,114 in U.S. dollars and 17.7% of the 1997 median gross income for U.S. practices is equal to $110,190.

Assets and Liabilties

The cash balance is relatively high in Canadian practices, with a median of 4.6% of gross income being carried in cash versus the U.S. median of 2.7%.

Accounts receivable seem to be a bit more of a problem in Canada than in the United States; the median accounts receivable as a percentage of gross income is 2.1% in Canada versus 1.8% in the United States.

As a percentage of gross income, practices in Canada carry slightly higher levels of inventory at a median of 3.8% of gross income compared to the United States at 3.4% of gross income.

The low current ratio tells us that practices in Canada have relatively more current debt versus current assets than U.S. practices. Their median current ratio is 0.56:1 where the U.S. median is 1.14:1. This means that practices in Canada have $.56 Canadian dollars in current assets for every $1 Canadian in current debt.

The quick ratio tells the same story, with a ratio of 0.15:1 compared to the U.S. median of 0.83:1. A lower quick ratio also reflects the fact that practices in Canada carry relatively higher levels of inventory than practices in the United States.

The median equity to asset ratio for practices in Canada is 0.35:1, which means that these practices own about 35% of their assets while the rest are financed outside the practice. The U.S. median is 0.56:1. However, this is not necessarily an unfavorable comparison. Practices in Canada may be using more outside financing to free up cash for other uses.

	Yes	No	Total
Practice open 24 hours	14	15	29
	48.3%	51.7%	100.0%

	Yes	No	Total
Hospital owned by practicing veterinarians who own their own hospitals	19	10	29
	65.5%	34.5%	100.0%

	Median	Average	Number of Responses
(If owned by practitioners) Number of shareholders	11	19.79	19

	Yes	No	Total
Have a nonveterinarian hospital manager/administrator	15	14	29
	52.0%	48.3%	100.0%

	Median	Average	Number of Responses
Average number of hospitals that refer to you	30	44.8	29

	Yes	No	Total
Lease space in hospital to specialists	7	21	28
	25.0%	75.0%	100.0%

Staff	25th Percentile	Median	Average	Your Data	75th Percentile	Number of Responses
Number of Full-time Equivalent Veterinarians	3.9	4.6	5.9		7.7	24
(If salaried) Average Yearly Salary per Veterinarian	$43,500	$47,550	$48,667		$49,839	16
(If commissioned) Percentage of Individual Gross Income Paid to Staff Veterinarians	22.0%	25.0%	25.6%		29.0%	17
Number of Full-time Equivalent Nonveterinarian Staff	6.3	11.8	16.7		21.3	28
Number of Non-veterinarian Staff per Veterinarian	2.3	3.3	3.3		3.9	22
Number of Transactions per Veterinarian	1,350	2,044	2,187		2,687	21
Average Transaction Charge (ATC)	$71.32	$112.12	$111.63		$140.38	24
Income per Veterinarian	$197,017	$235,437	$245,225		$280,791	23
Income						
Examination/Emergency Income as a Percentage of Total Gross Income	11.1%	16.3%	19.3%		28.4%	25
Injections Income as a Percentage of Total Gross Income	6.9%	9.0%	9.2%		12.1%	22
Fluids Income as a Percentage of Total Gross Income	3.8%	6.0%	6.6%		9.4%	21
Bandage/Splint Income as a Percentage of Total Gross Income	0.6%	0.7%	1.0%		1.0%	18
Radiology Income as a Percentage of Total Gross Income	3.8%	7.6%	7.5%		10.6%	25
Laboratory Income as a Percentage of Total Gross Income	9.5%	11.5%	11.7%		12.6%	25
Hospitalization Income as a Percentage of Total Gross Income	5.2%	8.3%	10.2%		12.7%	24
Sedation/Anesthesia Income as a Percentage of Total Gross Income	3.9%	5.1%	5.3%		6.8%	22
Surgery Income as a Percentage of Total Gross Income	5.2%	7.9%	7.9%		10.5%	24
Pharmacy Income as a Percentage of Total Gross Income	4.8%	8.3%	11.5%		13.9%	24
Euthanasia/Cremation Income as a Percentage of Total Gross Income	2.4%	3.2%	3.2%		3.3%	19
Professional Services Income as a Percentage of Total Gross Income	2.5%	4.5%	8.2%		8.2%	23
Total Gross Income 1996	$509,520	$808,849	$1,003,634		$1,585,625	27
Total Gross Income 1997	$566,678	$906,494	$1,192,938		$1,648,058	29
Total Gross Income Growth Rate from 1996 to 1997	3.9%	7.0%	9.1%		12.1%	27
Expenses						
Drug and Medical Supply Expenses as a Percentage of Total Gross Income	8.3%	11.7%	11.5%		14.1%	28
Laboratory Expenses as a Percentage of Total Gross Income	1.2%	2.2%	2.5%		3.0%	24
Cremation Service Expenses as a Percentage of Total Gross Income	0.5%	0.9%	0.9%		1.4%	24
Salaries of Nonowner Veterinarians as a Percentage of Total Gross Income	13.8%	19.0%	19.1%		26.0%	26
Salaries of Nonveterinarian Staff as a Percentage of Total Gross Income	16.4%	19.3%	20.0%		23.0%	28
Salaries of Hospital Manager/Administrator as a Percentage of Total Gross Income	2.2%	3.0%	3.4%		4.0%	21
Total Salaries of Nonveterinarian Staff/Managers as a Percentage of Total Gross Income	18.4%	21.8%	22.7%		25.6%	24
Employee Benefit Program Expenses as a Percentage of Total Gross Income	1.6%	1.8%	2.4%		3.2%	22
Rent/Lease of Facility Expenses as a Percentage of Total Gross Income	3.2%	3.8%	4.6%		5.6%	26
Total Expenses as a Percentage of Total Gross Income	71.6%	80.6%	81.2%		93.1%	26
Net Income Before Owner Compensation as a Percentage of Total Gross Income	6.9%	19.4%	18.8%		28.4%	26
Total Salaries/Draw Paid to Owners as a Percentage of Total Gross Income	3.2%	13.0%	13.2%		19.2%	25

Assets and Liabilities	25th Percentile	Median	Average	Your Data	75th Percentile	Number of Responses
Cash and Cash Equivalents	$10,000	$48,000	$65,559	________	$91,436	27
Accounts Receivable	$3,000	$10,476	$20,240	________	$30,276	25
Accounts Receivable as a Percentage of Total Gross Income	0.6%	1.3%	1.6%	________	2.1%	25
Inventory	$5,000	$12,457	$20,593	________	$31,950	26
Current Assets	$65,460	$124,500	$268,194	________	$320,916	28
Total Assets	$141,856	$221,692	$411,039	________	$567,043	28
Current Liabilities	$5,000	$42,358	$123,094	________	$176,861	26
Total Liabilities	$19,697	$103,532	$226,128	________	$354,000	27
Total Equity	$26,677	$107,740	$193,653	________	$293,953	27
Current Ratio	1.1	1.4	2.2	________	2.2	25
Quick Ratio	0.9	1.4	2.1	________	2.7	23
Equity to Asset Ratio	0.1	0.3	0.3	________	0.5	24

Emergency and Critical Care Practice Analysis

Twenty-nine emergency/critical care practices responded to this survey. For any survey, there are varying levels of confidence in the results, depending on the number of responses. Twenty-nine responses represent a confidence level of 95% (±19%). This means you can feel comfortable the results for this analysis pertain to 95% of emergency/critical care practices with a margin of error of 19% for each data point.

There may be some variability in the data related to what type of emergency/critical care practices responded to the survey. A general practice that does emergency work at night is different from an after-hours only emergency practice. In addition, a practice with specialists may have different numbers from a practice with none. In a practice in which the same person who completes the exams also does all the surgeries, there may be a higher production per veterinarian than a practice where each specialist works only in his or her area of expertise.

General Information

Emergency/critical care practices have a significantly different function than the other practices surveyed. The data supports the hypothesis that emergency/critical care practices' expenses are very different than those of other practices.

A total of 20 emergency/critical care facilities responded to the survey. We asked several questions about the practices' nature to get a better idea about these practices' demographics. About half are open 24 hours a day. About two-thirds are owned by practicing veterinarians who own individual practices and also have an ownership interest in the emergency/critical care practice. The median number of shareholders in these practices is 11 and the average is 19.

About half of these emergency/critical care practices have a non-veterinarian practice manager or practice administrator. The median number of referring practices is 30 and the average is 45. One-quarter of these practices lease space to specialists.

Staff

The median number of full-time equivalent veterinarians is 4.6, with a median of 11.8 nonveterinarian staff per veterinarian. This translates to a median and an average of 3.3 nonveterinarian staff per veterinarian, which is not significantly different than the national figures.

Income

Emergency/critical care practices are bigger in terms of gross income than other practices we surveyed. The U.S. median for 1997 gross income is $622,541 and the emergency/critical care median is $906,494.

Emergency/critical care practices' gross incomes are growing about as fast (7.0%) as the U.S. median (7.5%).

We surveyed more income categories for emergency/critical care practices than for other practices. Laboratory income is about the same as the U.S. median at 11.5%, and is actually lower than that for the small animal practices, which have a median value of 12.6%. Radiology makes up a far greater percentage of income in emergency/critical care practices than in nonemergency/critical care practices, at a median of 7.6% versus 2.9%. (See pages 18–21 for data on all other gross income categories.)

Emergency practices' gross incomes are growing about as fast (7%) as the national median (7.5%).

Productivity

The median number of transactions per veterinarian is 2,044 and appears low compared to that of other practices (4,634). However, the average transaction charge (ATC) is $112.12 compared to the U.S. median of $59.76 (see page 30). The median gross income per veterinarian is $235,437, which is only about 84% of the U.S. median of $279,284.

Expenses

Drugs and medical supplies expense is much lower for emergency/critical care practices (11.7%) than the U.S. median of 15.6%. Emergency/critical care practices do not have to carry the full spectrum of drugs and supplies that other practices do, which results in lower drug expenses.

The median laboratory expense is 2.2%, which is lower than the U.S. median of 2.5%. The median markup on laboratory is 423% compared to the U.S. median of 350% (see page 36). This may be because virtually all lab work is done in-house in emergency practices.

Emergency/critical care and critical care practices pay a median of 19.3% of their gross income to nonveterinarian staff compared to the U.S. median of 20.0%. In many cases, emergency/critical care practices do not have practice owners working in the practice. Even if the owner does work in the practice, associate veterinarians must cover many hours. Since half of these practices are open 24 hours a day, it is not surprising that their associate veterinarian expense is so much higher than those of other practices.

For veterinarians paid on salary, the numbers do not vary much. The 25th percentile is $43,500, the median is $47,550, the average is $48,667, and the 75th percentile is $49,839. For those paid as a percentage of personal production, the median and the average are both about 25%. The 75th percentile is 29%. Obviously, the percentage of production is much higher in emergency/critical care practices than in other practices, where the typical number is 20–22%.

There are at least three possible reasons why emergency veterinarians get paid more (as a percentage of personal production) than veterinarians in general practices. First, emergency veterinarians have to work the hours no one else wants to work: nights, weekends, and holidays. Second, the job can be significantly more stressful than general practices. Third, emergency veterinarians may need more specialized skills and education.

Salaries of nonveterinarian staff of 19.3% of gross income are similar to the U.S. median of 20.0%.

The median employee benefits program expense percentage appears to be in line with that of other practices at 1.8% versus 2.0%.

The median rent/lease of facility expense percentage is lower for the emergency/critical care practices (3.8% versus the U.S. median of 5.7%). This may be because relatively more emergency/critical care practices are located in strip mall locations with lower rent than other types of space.

The median total expense percentage of 80.6% is significantly higher than the U.S. median of 75.1% (see page 48). This higher median total expense percentage is because emergency/critical care practices use a higher number of nonowner veterinarians than nonemergency practices.

Owner Compensation

The median net income before owner compensation is 19.4% compared to the U.S. median of 24.9%. The median total salaries/draw paid to owners as a percentage of gross income is 12.9% compared to the U.S. median of 17.7%.

These figures indicate that owners are taking home a median of $116,938 in emergency/critical care practices and $110,190 in nonemergency practices. Remember that this is not the "per owner" take home pay, since the average number of owners in a practice is about 1.5. In emergency/critical care practices owned by multiple shareholders, the dollars paid to owners is divided among a median of 11 shareholders.

Assets and Liabilities

Emergency/critical care practices maintain high median balances of cash ($48,000 or 5.3% of 1997 gross income versus the U.S. median of 2.7% of 1997 gross income). While emergency/critical care practices have relatively low accounts receivable (1.3% of gross income versus the U.S. median of 1.8%), we suspect they probably have much higher bad-debt expenses than other practices. Because we did not collect bad-debt figures this year, we cannot confirm this suspicion.

Inventory is lower than other practices at 1.4% of gross income ($12,457) compared to the U.S. median of 3.4% of gross income ($21,000). This makes sense since the drug and medical supply expenses were correspondingly low.

Strong current and quick ratios demonstrate that emergency/critical care practices are in good financial health when it comes to being able to cover current debt with current assets. The median current ratio for emergency/critical care practices is 1.41:1 while the U.S. median is 1.14:1. The median quick ratio is 1.38:1 versus the U.S. median of 0.83:1.

The equity to asset ratio does not compare as favorably, at a median of 0.29:1 versus the U.S. median of 0.56:1. This figure shows that such practices require larger amounts of capital and equipment in order to operate as compared to general practices. Emergency practices may have different equipment than general practices and also need to have large quantities of certain types of equipment. For example, an emergency practice may need ten infusion pumps on hand to care for multiple patients. The requirement for additional equipment is also magnified if the practice uses specialists.

Appendix

Staff	25th Percentile	Median	Average	Your Data	75th Percentile	Number of Responses
Number of Full-time Equivalent Veterinarians	1.3	2.0	2.4	________	3.0	584
Number of Full-time Equivalent Nonveterinarian Staff	4.0	6.0	7.6	________	9.8	580
Number of Nonveterinarian Staff per Veterinarian	2.3	3.0	3.2	________	4.0	578
Number of Transactions per Veterinarian	3,645	4,634	4,677	________	5,495	466
Average Transaction Charge (ATC)	$51.35	$59.76	$62.45	________	$71.26	480
Income per Veterinarian	$236,455	$279,284	$290,594	________	$327,807	581
Income						
Laboratory Income as a Percentage of Gross Income	9.2%	11.9%	11.9%	________	14.5%	503
Radiology Income as a Percentage of Gross Income	2.1%	2.9%	3.1%	________	3.8%	525
Dentistry Income as a Percentage of Gross Income	1.0%	1.5%	1.9%	________	2.3%	516
Ancillary Services Income as a Percentage of Gross Income	7.2%	13.3%	15.0%	________	21.3%	451
Gross Income 1996	$381,580	$576,299	$650,112	________	$805,591	551
Gross Income 1997	$412,000	$622,541	$707,704	________	$887,740	578
Gross Income Growth Rate From 1996 to 1997	3.5%	7.5%	8.8%	________	13.0%	556
Expenses						
Drug and Medical Supply Expenses as a Percentage of Gross Income	12.4%	15.6%	15.9%	________	18.8%	530
Laboratory Expenses as a Percentage of Gross Income	1.6%	2.5%	2.6%	________	3.4%	544
Ancillary Services Expenses as a Percentage of Gross Income	2.7%	4.4%	4.9%	________	6.5%	424
Salary Expenses of Nonowner Veterinarians as a Percentage of Gross Income	5.9%	8.4%	8.9%	________	12.0%	441
Salary Expenses of Nonveterinarian Staff as a Percentage of Gross Income	17.7%	20.0%	20.4%	________	22.6%	411
Employee Benefit Program Expenses as a Percentage of Gross Income	1.1%	2.0%	2.3%	________	3.2%	436
Rent/Lease of Facility Expenses as a Percentage of Gross Income	4.0%	5.7%	5.9%	________	7.7%	405
Total Expenses as a Percentage of Gross Income	66.0%	75.1%	74.9%	________	83.6%	453
Net Income Before Owner Compensation as a Percentage of Gross Income	16.4%	24.9%	25.1%	________	34.0%	453
Total Salaries/Draw Paid to Owners as a Percentage of Gross Income	11.8%	17.7%	18.7%	________	24.7%	540
Assets and Liabilities						
Cash and Cash Equivalents	$6,291	$16,549	$38,338	________	$40,204	544
Accounts Receivable	$4,522	$10,619	$19,626	________	$23,212	539
Accounts Receivable as a Percentage of Gross Income	0.9%	1.8%	2.3%	________	3.1%	523
Inventory	$12,533	$21,000	$30,442	________	$38,000	489
Current Assets	$43,111	$80,521	$117,422	________	$143,393	509
Total Assets	$70,977	$146,313	$228,699	________	$283,600	529
Current Liabilities	$8,596	$29,945	$53,146	________	$58,000	517
Total Liabilities	$20,000	$59,777	$123,683	________	$154,009	535
Total Equity	$18,875	$72,984	$125,215	________	$167,744	439
Current Ratio	0.7	1.1	2.4	________	2.4	447
Quick Ratio	0.3	0.8	1.8	________	1.9	404
Equity to Asset Ratio	0.1	0.6	0.5	________	0.8	520

Staff	25th Percentile	Median	Average	Your Data	75th Percentile	Number of Responses
Number of Full-time Equivalent Veterinarians	1.3	2.0	2.5	______	3.4	128
Number of Full-time Equivalent Nonveterinarian Staff	3.5	5.5	6.7	______	8.5	125
Number of Nonveterinarian Staff per Veterinarian	1.8	2.5	2.7	______	3.4	125
Number of Transactions per Veterinarian	3,519	4,026	4,432	______	5,280	96
Average Transaction Charge (ATC)	$48.83	$56.46	$61.07	______	$71.95	102
Income per Veterinarian	$212,382	$268,776	$268,785	______	$306,750	126
Income						
Laboratory Income as a Percentage of Gross Income	7.1%	9.6%	9.8%	______	11.8%	96
Radiology Income as a Percentage of Gross Income	1.6%	2.4%	2.6%	______	3.1%	108
Dentistry Income as a Percentage of Gross Income	0.8%	1.2%	1.6%	______	1.8%	106
Ancillary Services Income as a Percentage of Gross Income	7.0%	12.6%	14.0%	______	18.7%	87
Gross Income 1996	$372,202	$551,626	$620,820	______	$805,591	114
Gross Income 1997	$412,217	$599,638	$687,961	______	$869,847	122
Gross Income Growth Rate From 1996 to 1997	2.0%	6.5%	7.8%	______	13.0%	117
Expenses						
Drug and Medical Supply Expenses as a Percentage of Gross Income	15.5%	18.1%	18.5%	______	22.8%	101
Laboratory Expenses as a Percentage of Gross Income	1.4%	2.4%	2.4%	______	3.4%	116
Ancillary Services Expenses as a Percentage of Gross Income	2.4%	4.6%	4.8%	______	6.1%	85
Salary Expenses of Nonowner Veterinarians as a Percentage of Gross Income	5.7%	8.4%	8.7%	______	12.0%	93
Salary Expenses of Nonveterinarian Staff as a Percentage of Gross Income	17.4%	18.8%	19.8%	______	21.0%	79
Employee Benefit Program Expenses as a Percentage of Gross Income	1.1%	1.8%	2.1%	______	2.9%	97
Rent/Lease of Facility Expenses as a Percentage of Gross Income	3.3%	5.3%	5.3%	______	7.1%	84
Total Expenses as a Percentage of Gross Income	67.4%	76.0%	75.0%	______	82.6%	84
Net Income Before Owner Compensation as a Percentage of Gross Income	17.4%	24.0%	25.0%	______	32.6%	84
Total Salaries/Draw Paid to Owners as a Percentage of Gross Income	11.8%	18.2%	19.1%	______	25.4%	114
Assets and Liabilities						
Cash and Cash Equivalents	$4,801	$10,998	$29,463	______	$35,638	118
Accounts Receivable	$9,765	$21,863	$37,497	______	$41,000	115
Accounts Receivable as a Percentage of Gross Income	2.0%	3.6%	4.1%	______	5.7%	105
Inventory	$15,000	$25,264	$33,854	______	$43,682	110
Current Assets	$49,115	$91,742	$140,308	______	$183,700	109
Total Assets	$73,000	$155,647	$226,773	______	$300,000	114
Current Liabilities	$10,100	$30,655	$58,632	______	$64,080	112
Total Liabilities	$17,000	$55,000	$115,297	______	$129,739	119
Total Equity	$20,000	$82,239	$121,545	______	$182,888	102
Current Ratio	0.7	1.8	2.8	______	3.1	94
Quick Ratio	0.3	0.8	2.1	______	2.2	89
Equity to Asset Ratio	0.2	0.6	0.5	______	0.8	115

Staff	25th Percentile	Median	Average	Your Data	75th Percentile	Number of Responses
Number of Full-time Equivalent Veterinarians	1.3	2.0	2.4		3.0	467
Number of Full-time Equivalent Nonveterinarian Staff	4.0	6.0	7.8		10.0	466
Number of Nonveterinarian Staff per Veterinarian	2.5	3.1	3.3		4.0	464
Number of Transactions per Veterinarian	3,668	4,770	4,743		5,553	381
Average Transaction Charge (ATC)	$52.07	$60.42	$63.01		$71.26	389
Income per Veterinarian	$242,521	$281,399	$297,261		$333,428	466
Income						
Laboratory Income as a Percentage of Gross Income	9.9%	12.6%	12.5%		15.1%	418
Radiology Income as a Percentage of Gross Income	2.2%	2.9%	3.2%		3.8%	428
Dentistry Income as a Percentage of Gross Income	1.0%	1.6%	2.0%		2.5%	422
Ancillary Services Income as a Percentage of Gross Income	7.7%	13.5%	15.2%		21.5%	376
Gross Income 1996	$378,400	$577,529	$648,627		$800,288	448
Gross Income 1997	$402,222	$618,879	$704,157		$887,740	467
Gross Income Growth Rate From 1996 to 1997	3.6%	8.0%	9.2%		13.2%	451
Expenses						
Drug and Medical Supply Expenses as a Percentage of Gross Income	12.1%	14.8%	15.2%		18.0%	438
Laboratory Expenses as a Percentage of Gross Income	1.6%	2.6%	2.7%		3.5%	439
Ancillary Services Expenses as a Percentage of Gross Income	2.7%	4.5%	4.9%		6.6%	351
Salary Expenses of Nonowner Veterinarians as a Percentage of Gross Income	6.0%	8.3%	8.9%		11.9%	354
Salary Expenses of Nonveterinarian Staff as a Percentage of Gross Income	17.9%	20.0%	20.5%		23.0%	344
Employee Benefit Program Expenses as a Percentage of Gross Income	1.1%	2.0%	2.3%		3.2%	348
Rent/Lease of Facility Expenses as a Percentage of Gross Income	4.0%	5.8%	6.1%		7.9%	332
Total Expenses as a Percentage of Gross Income	65.1%	74.9%	75.0%		84.0%	377
Net Income Before Owner Compensation as a Percentage of Gross Income	16.0%	25.1%	25.1%		34.9%	377
Total Salaries/Draw Paid to Owners as a Percentage of Gross Income	11.7%	17.6%	18.6%		24.2%	434
Assets and Liabilities						
Cash and Cash Equivalents	$6,948	$17,501	$39,958		$40,204	436
Accounts Receivable	$4,000	$8,462	$14,469		$18,680	435
Accounts Receivable as a Percentage of Gross Income	0.8%	1.6%	1.9%		2.5%	429
Inventory	$11,038	$20,000	$28,868		$35,000	390
Current Assets	$39,112	$76,534	$108,184		$136,671	408
Total Assets	$67,787	$140,000	$224,866		$266,000	426
Current Liabilities	$7,279	$29,711	$50,313		$55,600	414
Total Liabilities	$21,603	$60,000	$124,151		$156,045	428
Total Equity	$16,765	$65,269	$122,417		$158,748	349
Current Ratio	0.6	1.1	2.3		2.2	359
Quick Ratio	0.3	0.8	1.7		1.8	320
Equity to Asset Ratio	0.1	0.5	0.5		0.9	417

Staff	25th Percentile	Median	Average	Your Data	75th Percentile	Number of Responses
Number of Full-time Equivalent Veterinarians	2.0	2.0	2.6	________	3.4	32
Number of Full-time Equivalent Nonveterinarian Staff	4.0	6.0	7.5	________	10.0	31
Number of Nonveterinarian Staff per Veterinarian	2.2	2.8	3.0	________	3.1	31
Number of Transactions per Veterinarian	3,889	4,905	5,177	________	6,249	23
Average Transaction Charge (ATC)	$49.83	$59.34	$60.47	________	$70.71	24
Income per Veterinarian	$241,884	$311,322	$296,674	________	$333,321	32
Income						
Laboratory Income as a Percentage of Gross Income	8.9%	11.4%	11.4%	________	13.7%	28
Radiology Income as a Percentage of Gross Income	2.3%	2.8%	3.0%	________	3.3%	28
Dentistry Income as a Percentage of Gross Income	0.9%	1.2%	1.7%	________	2.0%	27
Ancillary Services Income as a Percentage of Gross Income	9.4%	16.9%	17.1%	________	21.3%	23
Gross Income 1996	$450,493	$552,916	$734,332	________	$980,000	31
Gross Income 1997	$483,769	$598,000	$797,451	________	$1,054,000	31
Gross Income Growth Rate From 1996 to 1997	4.2%	10.1%	8.6%	________	13.6%	31
Expenses						
Drug and Medical Supply Expenses as a Percentage of Gross Income	13.9%	16.3%	16.2%	________	18.7%	31
Laboratory Expenses as a Percentage of Gross Income	1.4%	2.5%	2.5%	________	2.8%	30
Ancillary Services Expenses as a Percentage of Gross Income	4.0%	5.0%	6.0%	________	8.3%	21
Salary Expenses of Nonowner Veterinarians as a Percentage of Gross Income	4.3%	9.9%	9.2%	________	13.0%	26
Salary Expenses of Nonveterinarian Staff as a Percentage of Gross Income	20.3%	21.0%	21.4%	________	24.2%	20
Employee Benefit Program Expenses as a Percentage of Gross Income	1.9%	2.5%	2.7%	________	3.6%	25
Rent/Lease of Facility Expenses as a Percentage of Gross Income	3.9%	5.5%	5.5%	________	8.4%	23
Total Expenses as a Percentage of Gross Income	71.6%	81.3%	80.2%	________	89.6%	24
Net Income Before Owner Compensation as a Percentage of Gross Income	10.4%	18.7%	19.8%	________	28.4%	24
Total Salaries/Draw Paid to Owners as a Percentage of Gross Income	9.6%	16.7%	17.2%	________	26.2%	29
Assets and Liabilities						
Cash and Cash Equivalents	$5,876	$12,160	$27,204	________	$31,417	30
Accounts Receivable	$5,944	$13,262	$23,970	________	$25,641	31
Accounts Receivable as a Percentage of Gross Income	1.1%	2.0%	2.3%	________	3.8%	29
Inventory	$12,305	$29,050	$52,727	________	$59,919	24
Current Assets	$30,165	$69,904	$122,742	________	$171,768	26
Total Assets	$42,861	$88,704	$169,472	________	$317,754	25
Current Liabilities	$12,198	$29,606	$75,766	________	$91,503	28
Total Liabilities	$22,000	$58,392	$125,425	________	$203,492	27
Total Equity	($12,412)	$25,424	$45,934	________	$82,239	20
Current Ratio	0.7	1.1	2.1	________	2.2	23
Quick Ratio	0.4	0.5	1.0	________	0.9	18
Equity to Asset Ratio	0.0	0.2	0.3	________	0.6	24

Staff	25th Percentile	Median	Average	Your Data	75th Percentile	Number of Responses
Number of Full-time Equivalent Veterinarians	1.3	2.0	2.6		3.3	57
Number of Full-time Equivalent Nonveterinarian Staff	5.0	7.0	8.8		11.0	58
Number of Nonveterinarian Staff per Veterinarian	2.4	3.0	3.4		4.1	57
Number of Transactions per Veterinarian	3,870	4,521	4,715		5,598	43
Average Transaction Charge (ATC)	$56.47	$63.08	$66.79		$74.66	45
Income per Veterinarian	$253,542	$280,741	$302,203		$328,669	55
Income						
Laboratory Income as a Percentage of Gross Income	10.2%	12.7%	12.6%		14.9%	52
Radiology Income as a Percentage of Gross Income	2.2%	3.0%	3.2%		3.8%	52
Dentistry Income as a Percentage of Gross Income	0.8%	1.0%	1.4%		1.9%	51
Ancillary Services Income as a Percentage of Gross Income	5.7%	13.3%	14.9%		25.6%	46
Gross Income 1996	$412,813	$638,500	$737,063		$933,188	54
Gross Income 1997	$474,993	$676,525	$807,967		$1,034,531	56
Gross Income Growth Rate From 1996 to 1997	3.8%	8.4%	10.6%		12.6%	54
Expenses						
Drug and Medical Supply Expenses as a Percentage of Gross Income	10.5%	15.5%	14.8%		18.9%	54
Laboratory Expenses as a Percentage of Gross Income	1.9%	2.8%	2.8%		3.4%	53
Ancillary Services Expenses as a Percentage of Gross Income	2.4%	3.8%	4.6%		6.5%	45
Salary Expenses of Nonowner Veterinarians as a Percentage of Gross Income	6.6%	10.3%	10.4%		14.0%	47
Salary Expenses of Nonveterinarian Staff as a Percentage of Gross Income	17.4%	19.6%	20.5%		23.0%	40
Employee Benefit Program Expenses as a Percentage of Gross Income	1.3%	2.6%	2.5%		3.4%	45
Rent/Lease of Facility Expenses as a Percentage of Gross Income	3.9%	6.2%	5.8%		7.7%	36
Total Expenses as a Percentage of Gross Income	63.7%	74.8%	73.7%		83.4%	49
Net Income Before Owner Compensation as a Percentage of Gross Income	16.7%	25.2%	26.3%		36.3%	49
Total Salaries/Draw Paid to Owners as a Percentage of Gross Income	12.9%	21.2%	19.8%		25.0%	50
Assets and Liabilities						
Cash and Cash Equivalents	$5,524	$26,614	$41,182		$59,055	53
Accounts Receivable	$4,500	$10,000	$25,921		$24,929	54
Accounts Receivable as a Percentage of Gross Income	0.7%	1.5%	1.9%		2.7%	52
Inventory	$14,365	$26,534	$31,470		$36,025	47
Current Assets	$48,768	$89,738	$136,624		$160,000	46
Total Assets	$79,695	$180,916	$288,221		$316,478	49
Current Liabilities	$5,864	$26,000	$59,171		$58,000	47
Total Liabilities	$23,069	$74,893	$137,756		$183,919	48
Total Equity	$25,000	$109,400	$199,799		$215,301	37
Current Ratio	0.5	1.8	3.4		3.8	39
Quick Ratio	0.2	1.3	2.6		2.9	35
Equity to Asset Ratio	0.2	0.7	0.5		1.0	49

Staff	25th Percentile	Median	Average	Your Data	75th Percentile	Number of Responses
Number of Full-time Equivalent Veterinarians	1.3	2.0	2.2	______	3.0	76
Number of Full-time Equivalent Nonveterinarian Staff	4.5	6.5	7.2	______	8.8	76
Number of Nonveterinarian Staff per Veterinarian	2.5	3.1	3.3	______	4.0	76
Number of Transactions per Veterinarian	4,011	4,862	4,874	______	5,650	58
Average Transaction Charge (ATC)	$48.83	$56.51	$57.21	______	$63.60	61
Income per Veterinarian	$216,240	$279,284	$280,814	______	$317,979	76
Income						
Laboratory Income as a Percentage of Gross Income	10.5%	12.0%	12.3%	______	14.3%	62
Radiology Income as a Percentage of Gross Income	1.6%	2.3%	2.4%	______	3.0%	69
Dentistry Income as a Percentage of Gross Income	0.9%	1.2%	1.5%	______	1.9%	64
Ancillary Services Income as a Percentage of Gross Income	10.0%	12.6%	14.5%	______	18.5%	57
Gross Income 1996	$357,878	$515,320	$568,780	______	$748,000	74
Gross Income 1997	$367,751	$564,171	$619,454	______	$792,699	76
Gross Income Growth Rate From 1996 to 1997	3.0%	5.9%	7.7%	______	11.0%	74
Expenses						
Drug and Medical Supply Expenses as a Percentage of Gross Income	15.2%	18.5%	18.6%	______	21.8%	64
Laboratory Expenses as a Percentage of Gross Income	1.2%	2.0%	2.4%	______	3.4%	73
Ancillary Services Expenses as a Percentage of Gross Income	2.6%	4.0%	4.2%	______	5.4%	53
Salary Expenses of Nonowner Veterinarians as a Percentage of Gross Income	7.0%	8.2%	8.6%	______	11.7%	53
Salary Expenses of Nonveterinarian Staff as a Percentage of Gross Income	18.0%	19.5%	20.0%	______	21.7%	57
Employee Benefit Program Expenses as a Percentage of Gross Income	1.1%	1.8%	2.1%	______	2.8%	56
Rent/Lease of Facility Expenses as a Percentage of Gross Income	4.0%	5.4%	5.8%	______	8.3%	50
Total Expenses as a Percentage of Gross Income	64.7%	74.7%	73.0%	______	80.6%	63
Net Income Before Owner Compensation as a Percentage of Gross Income	19.4%	25.3%	27.0%	______	35.3%	63
Total Salaries/Draw Paid to Owners as a Percentage of Gross Income	11.6%	20.3%	20.3%	______	28.1%	69
Assets and Liabilities						
Cash and Cash Equivalents	$7,175	$15,500	$36,632	______	$42,588	75
Accounts Receivable	$5,000	$10,169	$17,084	______	$21,500	70
Accounts Receivable as a Percentage of Gross Income	0.9%	1.8%	2.6%	______	3.6%	68
Inventory	$13,000	$24,000	$28,909	______	$36,723	65
Current Assets	$42,632	$82,185	$123,804	______	$139,781	70
Total Assets	$65,003	$155,570	$226,103	______	$299,738	70
Current Liabilities	$9,380	$27,291	$44,345	______	$48,375	74
Total Liabilities	$12,854	$57,272	$114,037	______	$127,469	72
Total Equity	$29,867	$102,245	$130,867	______	$205,554	59
Current Ratio	0.8	1.1	2.6	______	2.3	64
Quick Ratio	0.5	1.1	2.3	______	1.8	55
Equity to Asset Ratio	0.0	0.6	0.5	______	0.9	68

Staff	25th Percentile	Median	Average	Your Data	75th Percentile	Number of Responses
Number of Full-time Equivalent Veterinarians	1.5	2.3	2.6	______	3.3	117
Number of Full-time Equivalent Nonveterinarian Staff	4.0	6.0	7.4	______	9.4	116
Number of Nonveterinarian Staff per Veterinarian	2.0	2.7	2.9	______	3.6	115
Number of Transactions per Veterinarian	3,298	4,180	4,523	______	5,453	98
Average Transaction Charge (ATC)	$50.79	$57.2	$60.5	______	$66.8	100
Income per Veterinarian	$228,766	$257,803	$268,788	______	$320,515	117
Income						
Laboratory Income as a Percentage of Gross Income	10.4%	13.4%	13.2%	______	15.9%	107
Radiology Income as a Percentage of Gross Income	2.0%	2.8%	2.9%	______	3.5%	109
Dentistry Income as a Percentage of Gross Income	0.9%	1.3%	1.9%	______	2.2%	108
Ancillary Services Income as a Percentage of Gross Income	5.7%	10.9%	12.7%	______	17.1%	102
Gross Income 1996	$396,100	$589,922	$642,194	______	$789,215	112
Gross Income 1997	$433,210	$654,790	$697,437	______	$860,097	116
Gross Income Growth Rate From 1996 to 1997	4.7%	8.2%	9.2%	______	13.2%	114
Expenses						
Drug and Medical Supply Expenses as a Percentage of Gross Income	12.5%	14.7%	15.9%	______	18.3%	111
Laboratory Expenses as a Percentage of Gross Income	2.0%	2.7%	2.8%	______	3.6%	113
Ancillary Services Expenses as a Percentage of Gross Income	2.5%	3.6%	4.0%	______	5.1%	89
Salary Expenses of Nonowner Veterinarians as a Percentage of Gross Income	6.3%	10.0%	9.6%	______	12.8%	92
Salary Expenses of Nonveterinarian Staff as a Percentage of Gross Income	17.7%	20.0%	19.8%	______	21.3%	80
Employee Benefit Program Expenses as a Percentage of Gross Income	1.5%	2.4%	2.6%	______	3.8%	92
Rent/Lease of Facility Expenses as a Percentage of Gross Income	4.1%	5.7%	6.1%	______	7.1%	77
Total Expenses as a Percentage of Gross Income	67.2%	75.4%	75.9%	______	83.0%	92
Net Income Before Owner Compensation as a Percentage of Gross Income	17.0%	24.6%	24.1%	______	32.8%	92
Total Salaries/Draw Paid to Owners as a Percentage of Gross Income	12.9%	18.5%	19.9%	______	27.2%	110
Assets and Liabilities						
Cash and Cash Equivalents	$5,959	$14,378	$33,522	______	$39,424	113
Accounts Receivable	$4,178	$8,449	$17,957	______	$21,000	109
Accounts Receivable as a Percentage of Gross Income	0.8%	1.6%	2.3%	______	3.4%	106
Inventory	$15,599	$24,000	$37,263	______	$49,346	103
Current Assets	$51,228	$87,136	$104,508	______	$134,521	100
Total Assets	$83,195	$139,918	$217,212	______	$264,495	108
Current Liabilities	$12,442	$38,530	$67,925	______	$82,374	106
Total Liabilities	$34,196	$66,679	$129,818	______	$154,009	110
Total Equity	$17,701	$72,147	$112,010	______	$164,000	87
Current Ratio	0.5	0.9	1.8	______	1.8	94
Quick Ratio	0.2	0.6	1.2	______	1.3	88
Equity to Asset Ratio	0.2	0.5	0.4	______	0.8	106

Staff	25th Percentile	Median	Average	Your Data	75th Percentile	Number of Responses
Number of Full-time Equivalent Veterinarians	1.3	2.0	2.3		3.3	48
Number of Full-time Equivalent Nonveterinarian Staff	3.8	5.0	6.5		8.0	48
Number of Nonveterinarian Staff per Veterinarian	1.8	2.7	2.8		3.3	48
Number of Transactions per Veterinarian	3,265	4,129	4,157		4,959	42
Average Transaction Charge (ATC)	$52.86	$55.91	$61.31		$66.38	43
Income per Veterinarian	$208,193	$252,517	$250,849		$296,062	48
Income						
Laboratory Income as a Percentage of Gross Income	10.0%	13.1%	12.7%		15.3%	42
Radiology Income as a Percentage of Gross Income	2.1%	2.9%	2.7%		3.5%	43
Dentistry Income as a Percentage of Gross Income	1.1%	1.6%	1.7%		2.2%	43
Ancillary Services Income as a Percentage of Gross Income	10.6%	14.5%	16.1%		21.9%	37
Gross Income 1996	$334,088	$510,250	$539,228		$694,335	45
Gross Income 1997	$342,487	$538,626	$583,119		$808,599	48
Gross Income Growth Rate From 1996 to 1997	3.5%	7.0%	9.2%		12.0%	46
Expenses						
Drug and Medical Supply Expenses as a Percentage of Gross Income	12.8%	14.4%	15.6%		18.1%	43
Laboratory Expenses as a Percentage of Gross Income	1.2%	2.3%	2.4%		3.7%	41
Ancillary Services Expenses as a Percentage of Gross Income	4.7%	5.9%	6.2%		7.6%	35
Salary Expenses of Nonowner Veterinarians as a Percentage of Gross Income	6.1%	8.1%	9.0%		12.3%	35
Salary Expenses of Nonveterinarian Staff as a Percentage of Gross Income	18.1%	19.2%	20.5%		23.1%	33
Employee Benefit Program Expenses as a Percentage of Gross Income	1.0%	1.7%	2.1%		3.2%	33
Rent/Lease of Facility Expenses as a Percentage of Gross Income	4.0%	5.5%	5.5%		6.6%	30
Total Expenses as a Percentage of Gross Income	67.3%	74.6%	73.2%		81.6%	37
Net Income Before Owner Compensation as a Percentage of Gross Income	18.4%	25.4%	26.8%		32.7%	37
Total Salaries/Draw Paid to Owners as a Percentage of Gross Income	15.6%	19.5%	20.9%		26.6%	44
Assets and Liabilities						
Cash and Cash Equivalents	$3,808	$12,590	$27,429		$33,000	43
Accounts Receivable	$3,335	$12,339	$25,676		$31,100	44
Accounts Receivable as a Percentage of Gross Income	1.1%	2.7%	3.4%		5.1%	43
Inventory	$10,000	$24,569	$29,853		$47,536	43
Current Assets	$41,570	$72,663	$115,870		$137,244	44
Total Assets	$76,823	$148,201	$210,429		$255,653	46
Current Liabilities	$7,279	$21,215	$36,799		$49,623	42
Total Liabilities	$14,000	$41,400	$90,317		$116,555	46
Total Equity	$29,846	$69,543	$129,981		$168,847	42
Current Ratio	1.0	1.9	3.7		3.6	40
Quick Ratio	0.3	1.3	2.7		2.9	39
Equity to Asset Ratio	0.3	0.8	0.6		1.0	45

Staff	25th Percentile	Median	Average	Your Data	75th Percentile	Number of Responses
Number of Full-time Equivalent Veterinarians	1.0	2.1	1.9	________	2.5	6
Number of Full-time Equivalent Nonveterinarian Staff	3.5	6.3	6.3	________	7.5	6
Number of Nonveterinarian Staff per Veterinarian	2.1	3.1	3.3	________	3.8	6
Number of Transactions per Veterinarian	4,059	4,792	4,394	________	5,054	4
Average Transaction Charge (ATC)	$48.63	$56.18	$54.03	________	$57.39	4
Income per Veterinarian	$233,022	$237,347	$287,488	________	$290,010	6
Income						
Laboratory Income as a Percentage of Gross Income	4.0%	6.2%	5.9%	________	6.2%	5
Radiology Income as a Percentage of Gross Income	1.8%	3.0%	3.3%	________	5.6%	6
Dentistry Income as a Percentage of Gross Income	1.5%	1.7%	1.8%	________	2.5%	6
Ancillary Services Income as a Percentage of Gross Income	6.7%	12.3%	16.3%	________	25.6%	5
Gross Income 1996	$381,270	$517,100	$572,477	________	$757,304	5
Gross Income 1997	$228,025	$499,497	$546,706	________	$771,427	6
Gross Income Growth Rate From 1996 to 1997	1.9%	13.6%	10.5%	________	15.8%	5
Expenses						
Drug and Medical Supply Expenses as a Percentage of Gross Income	9.9%	10.0%	12.3%	________	11.8%	5
Laboratory Expenses as a Percentage of Gross Income	1.2%	2.6%	2.1%	________	2.6%	6
Ancillary Services Expenses as a Percentage of Gross Income	2.0%	7.3%	8.1%	________	13.2%	4
Salary Expenses of Nonowner Veterinarians as a Percentage of Gross Income	6.9%	6.9%	6.8%	________	6.9%	3
Salary Expenses of Nonveterinarian Staff as a Percentage of Gross Income	16.1%	20.7%	19.4%	________	20.7%	5
Employee Benefit Program Expenses as a Percentage of Gross Income	0.3%	1.7%	1.4%	________	2.1%	5
Rent/Lease of Facility Expenses as a Percentage of Gross Income	5.7%	9.5%	7.8%	________	9.5%	5
Total Expenses as a Percentage of Gross Income	67.4%	80.0%	77.6%	________	81.5%	5
Net Income Before Owner Compensation as a Percentage of Gross Income	18.5%	20.0%	22.4%	________	32.6%	5
Total Salaries/Draw Paid to Owners as a Percentage of Gross Income	10.7%	10.7%	16.3%	________	20.1%	6
Assets and Liabilities						
Cash and Cash Equivalents	$7,600	$13,843	$16,999	________	$29,322	6
Accounts Receivable	$13,785	$22,542	$30,739	________	$48,664	6
Accounts Receivable as a Percentage of Gross Income	4.8%	6.3%	5.6%	________	6.4%	6
Inventory	$20,000	$32,965	$36,809	________	$42,628	5
Current Assets	$36,405	$109,935	$102,764	________	$161,559	6
Total Assets	$50,800	$172,283	$146,800	________	$203,437	6
Current Liabilities	$7,451	$17,751	$39,558	________	$56,928	6
Total Liabilities	$9,383	$109,100	$76,652	________	$119,861	5
Total Equity	$18,569	$32,100	$64,508	________	$134,185	5
Current Ratio	1.1	1.1	2.6	________	2.8	5
Quick Ratio	0.6	0.6	1.8	________	2.1	5
Equity to Asset Ratio	0.2	0.5	0.5	________	1.0	5

Staff	25th Percentile	Median	Average	Your Data	75th Percentile	Number of Responses
Number of Full-time Equivalent Veterinarians	1.2	2.0	2.1		2.5	63
Number of Full-time Equivalent Nonveterinarian Staff	3.5	5.5	7.1		8	62
Number of Nonveterinarian Staff per Veterinarian	2.5	3.5	3.3		4	62
Number of Transactions per Veterinarian	3,365	4,570	4,466		5,079	48
Average Transaction Charge (ATC)	$50.66	$57.79	$61.78		$73.51	47
Income per Veterinarian	$216,875	$276,461	$270,806		$311,579	63
Income						
Laboratory Income as a Percentage of Gross Income	8.8%	11.3%	11.4%		14.8%	56
Radiology Income as a Percentage of Gross Income	1.6%	2.6%	3.0%		4.0%	60
Dentistry Income as a Percentage of Gross Income	1.3%	2.3%	2.9%		2.9%	58
Ancillary Services Income as a Percentage of Gross Income	6.6%	13.4%	14.3%		21.4%	50
Gross Income 1996	$342,826	$461,021	$527,538		$607,650	56
Gross Income 1997	$344,716	$545,113	$586,628		$684,827	62
Gross Income Growth Rate From 1996 to 1997	1.2%	6.3%	7.1%		10.6%	56
Expenses						
Drug and Medical Supply Expenses as a Percentage of Gross Income	10.3%	14.1%	14.5%		17.8%	55
Laboratory Expenses as a Percentage of Gross Income	1.0%	2.2%	2.5%		3.8%	60
Ancillary Services Expenses as a Percentage of Gross Income	2.7%	4.5%	5.0%		7.1%	50
Salary Expenses of Nonowner Veterinarians as a Percentage of Gross Income	5.3%	7.2%	8.3%		10.7%	43
Salary Expenses of Nonveterinarian Staff as a Percentage of Gross Income	18.0%	21.0%	21.4%		24.1%	40
Employee Benefit Program Expenses as a Percentage of Gross Income	1.3%	2.4%	2.3%		2.9%	45
Rent/Lease of Facility Expenses as a Percentage of Gross Income	3.5%	4.8%	5.7%		7.7%	47
Total Expenses as a Percentage of Gross Income	62.0%	71.5%	72.4%		82.1%	47
Net Income Before Owner Compensation as a Percentage of Gross Income	17.9%	28.5%	27.7%		38.1%	47
Total Salaries/Draw Paid to Owners as a Percentage of Gross Income	13.0%	17.7%	18.4%		22.9%	57
Assets and Liabilities						
Cash and Cash Equivalents	$6,000	$17,979	$27,981		$35,462	58
Accounts Receivable	$4,500	$11,220	$14,503		$21,000	55
Accounts Receivable as a Percentage of Gross Income	1.1%	2.0%	2.2%		2.9%	53
Inventory	$12,000	$17,425	$23,373		$24,000	55
Current Assets	$37,963	$76,691	$109,222		$177,918	58
Total Assets	$57,177	$128,651	$204,829		$241,686	56
Current Liabilities	$2,505	$12,500	$28,017		$33,361	53
Total Liabilities	$10,736	$31,804	$91,092		$66,380	57
Total Equity	$25,905	$66,325	$128,953		$168,589	50
Current Ratio	0.9	1.7	3.0		3.3	44
Quick Ratio	0.4	1.6	2.4		2.4	41
Equity to Asset Ratio	0.1	0.8	0.6		0.9	56

Staff	25th Percentile	Median	Average	Your Data	75th Percentile	Number of Responses
Number of Full-time Equivalent Veterinarians	1.5	2.0	2.5	________	3.2	29
Number of Full-time Equivalent Nonveterinarian Staff	5.0	7.0	7.3	________	9.8	29
Number of Nonveterinarian Staff per Veterinarian	2.0	2.7	2.9	________	3.5	29
Number of Transactions per Veterinarian	2,616	3,885	4,316	________	5,354	21
Average Transaction Charge (ATC)	$49.32	$61.53	$64.20	________	$74.78	22
Income per Veterinarian	$227,069	$270,185	$275,841	________	$284,240	29
Income						
Laboratory Income as a Percentage of Gross Income	5.9%	8.9%	9.3%	________	12.0%	22
Radiology Income as a Percentage of Gross Income	2.3%	3.1%	3.4%	________	4.4%	22
Dentistry Income as a Percentage of Gross Income	1.4%	2.1%	2.1%	________	2.6%	24
Ancillary Services Income as a Percentage of Gross Income	9.4%	17.6%	15.5%	________	18.8%	20
Gross Income 1996	$377,790	$572,339	$579,223	________	$790,334	28
Gross Income 1997	$416,000	$646,157	$685,131	________	$887,740	29
Gross Income Growth Rate From 1996 to 1997	3.0%	12.7%	10.3%	________	15.0%	28
Expenses						
Drug and Medical Supply Expenses as a Percentage of Gross Income	13.3%	15.8%	17.2%	________	19.2%	27
Laboratory Expenses as a Percentage of Gross Income	1.7%	2.4%	2.4%	________	2.7%	26
Ancillary Services Expenses as a Percentage of Gross Income	2.5%	5.2%	4.6%	________	5.8%	18
Salary Expenses of Nonowner Veterinarians as a Percentage of Gross Income	4.9%	8.1%	7.9%	________	10.4%	22
Salary Expenses of Nonveterinarian Staff as a Percentage of Gross Income	16.2%	18.2%	19.9%	________	24.2%	19
Employee Benefit Program Expenses as a Percentage of Gross Income	1.2%	2.3%	2.4%	________	4.0%	21
Rent/Lease of Facility Expenses as a Percentage of Gross Income	3.6%	4.6%	4.9%	________	6.3%	22
Total Expenses as a Percentage of Gross Income	66.8%	68.5%	71.5%	________	75.5%	16
Net Income Before Owner Compensation as a Percentage of Gross Income	24.5%	31.5%	28.5%	________	33.2%	16
Total Salaries/Draw Paid to Owners as a Percentage of Gross Income	5.4%	11.5%	14.1%	________	22.0%	27
Assets and Liabilities						
Cash and Cash Equivalents	$10,000	$35,000	$39,325	________	$70,000	25
Accounts Receivable	$8,000	$14,598	$21,899	________	$37,405	25
Accounts Receivable as a Percentage of Gross Income	1.0%	1.9%	2.8%	________	4.6%	24
Inventory	$8,332	$15,824	$19,832	________	$25,277	25
Current Assets	$49,115	$81,898	$115,646	________	$149,353	25
Total Assets	$82,300	$149,631	$246,046	________	$346,000	25
Current Liabilities	$13,739	$37,066	$53,559	________	$89,000	25
Total Liabilities	$15,371	$59,968	$111,159	________	$140,000	26
Total Equity	$18,383	$82,000	$138,142	________	$148,690	24
Current Ratio	0.4	1.3	1.9	________	2.2	21
Quick Ratio	0.1	0.7	1.5	________	2.1	20
Equity to Asset Ratio	0.2	0.7	0.5	________	1.0	25

Staff	25th Percentile	Median	Average	Your Data	75th Percentile	Number of Responses
Number of Full-time Equivalent Veterinarians	1.3	2.6	2.6	______	3.8	28
Number of Full-time Equivalent Nonveterinarian Staff	4.0	7.0	8.8	______	11.8	28
Number of Nonveterinarian Staff per Veterinarian	2.5	3.5	3.3	______	4.0	28
Number of Transactions per Veterinarian	3,755	4,614	4,700	______	5,316	27
Average Transaction Charge (ATC)	$53.80	$62.71	$67.40	______	$73.56	28
Income per Veterinarian	$268,776	$312,632	$337,789	______	$346,000	28
Income						
Laboratory Income as a Percentage of Gross Income	7.8%	10.9%	10.4%	______	12.2%	22
Radiology Income as a Percentage of Gross Income	3.1%	3.8%	3.9%	______	4.4%	26
Dentistry Income as a Percentage of Gross Income	1.3%	1.8%	2.2%	______	2.4%	26
Ancillary Services Income as a Percentage of Gross Income	9.8%	12.9%	14.2%	______	19.4%	24
Gross Income 1996	$400,297	$684,694	$783,229	______	$1,023,895	26
Gross Income 1997	$435,585	$860,000	$893,332	______	$1,104,260	28
Gross Income Growth Rate From 1996 to 1997	6.0%	8.1%	10.7%	______	11.1%	26
Expenses						
Drug and Medical Supply Expenses as a Percentage of Gross Income	10.5%	12.2%	12.9%	______	15.3%	25
Laboratory Expenses as a Percentage of Gross Income	1.9%	2.5%	2.6%	______	3.7%	27
Ancillary Services Expenses as a Percentage of Gross Income	3.7%	4.7%	5.8%	______	7.3%	23
Salary Expenses of Nonowner Veterinarians as a Percentage of Gross Income	7.1%	10.4%	9.3%	______	12.5%	22
Salary Expenses of Nonveterinarian Staff as a Percentage of Gross Income	17.4%	18.6%	20.8%	______	26.3%	21
Employee Benefit Program Expenses as a Percentage of Gross Income	0.8%	1.1%	1.6%	______	2.6%	21
Rent/Lease of Facility Expenses as a Percentage of Gross Income	5.9%	7.6%	7.5%	______	9.3%	21
Total Expenses as a Percentage of Gross Income	67.8%	82.4%	78.9%	______	87.8%	23
Net Income Before Owner Compensation as a Percentage of Gross Income	12.2%	17.6%	21.1%	______	32.2%	23
Total Salaries/Draw Paid to Owners as a Percentage of Gross Income	9.1%	15.4%	17.7%	______	24.8%	26
Assets and Liabilities						
Cash and Cash Equivalents	$9,566	$16,050	$41,279	______	$40,000	25
Accounts Receivable	$10,000	$16,449	$26,554	______	$40,400	27
Accounts Receivable as a Percentage of Gross Income	1.4%	2.1%	2.7%	______	2.9%	25
Inventory	$11,527	$25,250	$36,945	______	$53,187	21
Current Assets	$32,625	$89,527	$109,583	______	$150,000	24
Total Assets	$60,113	$103,574	$222,264	______	$238,297	27
Current Liabilities	$4,407	$23,887	$53,701	______	$43,291	26
Total Liabilities	$23,575	$45,000	$151,344	______	$168,971	27
Total Equity	$13,564	$49,141	$91,184	______	$105,249	21
Current Ratio	0.9	2.7	4.2	______	4.6	21
Quick Ratio	0.5	1.5	2.2	______	2.8	18
Equity to Asset Ratio	0.1	0.6	0.3	______	0.6	27

Staff	25th Percentile	Median	Average	Your Data	75th Percentile	Number of Responses
Number of Full-time Equivalent Veterinarians	1.0	2.0	2.3		3.0	57
Number of Full-time Equivalent Nonveterinarian Staff	4.3	7.0	8.7		11.0	56
Number of Nonveterinarian Staff per Veterinarian	2.9	3.3	3.7		4.5	56
Number of Transactions per Veterinarian	3,853	5,133	5,151		6,188	43
Average Transaction Charge (ATC)	$46.81	$55.87	$56.78		$64.28	46
Income per Veterinarian	$245,154	$294,645	$304,771		$358,364	57
Income						
Laboratory Income as a Percentage of Gross Income	8.7%	11.6%	10.9%		13.4%	46
Radiology Income as a Percentage of Gross Income	1.8%	2.3%	2.4%		2.9%	49
Dentistry Income as a Percentage of Gross Income	0.9%	1.4%	1.7%		1.9%	46
Ancillary Services Income as a Percentage of Gross Income	6.7%	17.8%	17.6%		25.4%	37
Gross Income 1996	$345,397	$550,000	$644,267		$894,658	55
Gross Income 1997	$375,000	$630,061	$711,935		$1,016,975	57
Gross Income Growth Rate From 1996 to 1997	3.6%	11.3%	10.8%		15.4%	55
Expenses						
Drug and Medical Supply Expenses as a Percentage of Gross Income	13.2%	17.6%	17.2%		20.6%	50
Laboratory Expenses as a Percentage of Gross Income	1.0%	1.7%	1.8%		2.4%	50
Ancillary Services Expenses as a Percentage of Gross Income	3.6%	6.1%	6.2%		8.2%	36
Salary Expenses of Nonowner Veterinarians as a Percentage of Gross Income	5.6%	6.7%	7.3%		8.3%	44
Salary Expenses of Nonveterinarian Staff as a Percentage of Gross Income	17.7%	19.8%	20.2%		21.4%	44
Employee Benefit Program Expenses as a Percentage of Gross Income	0.7%	2.2%	2.2%		3.2%	38
Rent/Lease of Facility Expenses as a Percentage of Gross Income	3.7%	5.9%	6.1%		8.5%	46
Total Expenses as a Percentage of Gross Income	67.3%	74.6%	74.1%		82.6%	45
Net Income Before Owner Compensation as a Percentage of Gross Income	17.4%	25.5%	25.9%		32.7%	45
Total Salaries/Draw Paid to Owners as a Percentage of Gross Income	10.3%	17.7%	17.9%		21.6%	55
Assets and Liabilities						
Cash and Cash Equivalents	$6,337	$13,346	$66,271		$31,472	52
Accounts Receivable	$2,652	$8,690	$15,626		$16,000	54
Accounts Receivable as a Percentage of Gross Income	0.7%	1.3%	1.8%		2.3%	53
Inventory	$9,200	$19,633	$23,667		$33,231	50
Current Assets	$39,424	$56,947	$119,126		$135,165	50
Total Assets	$48,621	$133,277	$236,140		$267,793	53
Current Liabilities	$7,000	$32,452	$55,385		$60,000	50
Total Liabilities	$30,254	$72,350	$124,950		$193,000	51
Total Equity	$5,900	$61,202	$139,195		$167,000	41
Current Ratio	0.7	1.4	2.5		3.1	44
Quick Ratio	0.4	0.9	2.0		2.7	42
Equity to Asset Ratio	0.4	0.7	0.5		0.8	51

Staff	25th Percentile	Median	Average	Your Data	75th Percentile	Number of Responses
Number of Full-time Equivalent Veterinarians	1.2	1.8	2.4	________	3.0	29
Number of Full-time Equivalent Nonveterinarian Staff	4.0	6.0	7.3	________	9.0	28
Number of Nonveterinarian Staff per Veterinarian	2.5	2.9	2.9	________	3.3	28
Number of Transactions per Veterinarian	3,577	4,780	4,667	________	5,500	20
Average Transaction Charge (ATC)	$61.52	$73.44	$72.79	________	$84.84	20
Income per Veterinarian	$280,813	$319,369	$339,126	________	$420,417	28
Income						
Laboratory Income as a Percentage of Gross Income	8.1%	10.9%	10.6%	________	11.5%	23
Radiology Income as a Percentage of Gross Income	3.2%	4.5%	4.8%	________	6.4%	24
Dentistry Income as a Percentage of Gross Income	1.2%	2.2%	2.3%	________	3.3%	24
Ancillary Services Income as a Percentage of Gross Income	9.9%	12.3%	14.7%	________	21.5%	19
Gross Income 1996	$450,163	$597,763	$785,343	________	$878,234	28
Gross Income 1997	$488,421	$652,332	$841,639	________	$898,480	28
Gross Income Growth Rate From 1996 to 1997	3.1%	6.3%	7.2%	________	10.9%	29
Expenses						
Drug and Medical Supply Expenses as a Percentage of Gross Income	15.9%	16.7%	17.4%	________	20.5%	26
Laboratory Expenses as a Percentage of Gross Income	2.6%	3.0%	3.0%	________	3.6%	27
Ancillary Services Expenses as a Percentage of Gross Income	2.6%	4.2%	4.3%	________	5.8%	19
Salary Expenses of Nonowner Veterinarians as a Percentage of Gross Income	5.9%	6.1%	7.7%	________	12.4%	22
Salary Expenses of Nonveterinarian Staff as a Percentage of Gross Income	18.4%	20.6%	20.7%	________	22.0%	20
Employee Benefit Program Expenses as a Percentage of Gross Income	0.7%	1.1%	1.4%	________	2.0%	21
Rent/Lease of Facility Expenses as a Percentage of Gross Income	4.1%	5.7%	6.0%	________	6.6%	14
Total Expenses as a Percentage of Gross Income	64.0%	74.4%	74.8%	________	85.9%	18
Net Income Before Owner Compensation as a Percentage of Gross Income	14.1%	25.6%	25.2%	________	36.0%	18
Total Salaries/Draw Paid to Owners as a Percentage of Gross Income	13.1%	17.8%	19.7%	________	25.1%	27
Assets and Liabilities						
Cash and Cash Equivalents	$13,468	$22,052	$71,494	________	$33,217	25
Accounts Receivable	$8,462	$14,544	$18,722	________	$24,374	25
Accounts Receivable as a Percentage of Gross Income	1.1%	1.8%	2.2%	________	2.9%	25
Inventory	$12,000	$17,059	$24,007	________	$28,259	23
Current Assets	$49,461	$104,078	$146,856	________	$233,088	23
Total Assets	$78,750	$379,032	$365,704	________	$532,417	26
Current Liabilities	$6,820	$37,294	$68,301	________	$70,265	22
Total Liabilities	$25,264	$190,188	$251,818	________	$433,326	25
Total Equity	$60,014	$95,531	$150,613	________	$240,658	21
Current Ratio	0.9	1.1	1.8	________	2.1	19
Quick Ratio	0.6	1.0	1.3	________	1.0	17
Equity to Asset Ratio	0.1	0.3	0.4	________	0.5	26

Staff	25th Percentile	Median	Average	Your Data	75th Percentile	Number of Responses
Number of Full-time Equivalent Veterinarians	1.3	2.0	2.3		3.0	21
Number of Full-time Equivalent Nonveterinarian Staff	4.0	6.0	8.0		10.0	21
Number of Nonveterinarian Staff per Veterinarian	2.9	3.3	3.5		4.0	21
Number of Transactions per Veterinarian	3,464	5,086	4,984		5,895	18
Average Transaction Charge (ATC)	$65.56	$71.70	$72.09		$80.79	19
Income per Veterinarian	$242,000	$380,157	$359,417		$456,015	21
Income						
Laboratory Income as a Percentage of Gross Income	8.9%	12.8%	11.9%		14.2%	18
Radiology Income as a Percentage of Gross Income	3.4%	4.4%	4.4%		5.2%	18
Dentistry Income as a Percentage of Gross Income	1.1%	2.0%	2.0%		2.3%	18
Ancillary Services Income as a Percentage of Gross Income	7.7%	10.3%	17.8%		30.1%	15
Gross Income 1996	$469,000	$715,000	$841,417		$1,092,426	19
Gross Income 1997	$475,196	$726,000	$813,823		$990,738	21
Gross Income Growth Rate From 1996 to 1997	–2.5%	2.9%	0.95%		7.7%	19
Expenses						
Drug and Medical Supply Expenses as a Percentage of Gross Income	9.9%	14.7%	13.8%		16.4%	21
Laboratory Expenses as a Percentage of Gross Income	2.7%	3.2%	3.4%		4.0%	19
Ancillary Services Expenses as a Percentage of Gross Income	2.4%	3.6%	4.9%		5.5%	13
Salary Expenses of Nonowner Veterinarians as a Percentage of Gross Income	4.4%	7.7%	8.2%		9.8%	17
Salary Expenses of Nonveterinarian Staff as a Percentage of Gross Income	17.4%	17.6%	19.1%		21.0%	18
Employee Benefit Program Expenses as a Percentage of Gross Income	1.4%	2.1%	2.8%		5.4%	15
Rent/Lease of Facility Expenses as a Percentage of Gross Income	3.2%	5.7%	5.8%		6.7%	17
Total Expenses as a Percentage of Gross Income	70.8%	74.5%	75.7%		81.4%	19
Net Income Before Owner Compensation as a Percentage of Gross Income	18.6%	25.5%	24.3%		29.2%	19
Total Salaries/Draw Paid to Owners as a Percentage of Gross Income	9.5%	17.2%	16.4%		22.8%	20
Assets and Liabilities						
Cash and Cash Equivalents	$9,791	$14,500	$27,723		$33,000	19
Accounts Receivable	$3,712	$9,348	$16,496		$25,352	20
Accounts Receivable as a Percentage of Gross Income	0.8%	1.3%	2.0%		2.9%	20
Inventory	$16,000	$19,675	$26,498		$28,000	14
Current Assets	$55,888	$97,092	$119,782		$145,959	19
Total Assets	$107,660	$214,088	$190,449		$246,519	20
Current Liabilities	$10,850	$29,927	$62,978		$80,810	20
Total Liabilities	$24,000	$127,072	$121,992		$219,743	21
Total Equity	$2,181	$58,822	$79,290		$145,224	16
Current Ratio	0.5	0.9	1.8		1.7	18
Quick Ratio	0.2	0.8	1.5		1.5	14
Equity to Asset Ratio	0.0	0.4	0.3		0.7	20

Staff	25th Percentile	Median	Average	Your Data	75th Percentile	Number of Responses
Number of Full-time Equivalent Veterinarians	1.0	1.0	1.0	______	1.0	117
Number of Full-time Equivalent Nonveterinarian Staff	2.0	3.0	3.4	______	4.0	114
Number of Nonveterinarian Staff per Veterinarian	2.0	3.0	3.4	______	4.0	114
Number of Transactions per Veterinarian	3,885	5,012	5,362	______	6,905	82
Average Transaction Charge (ATC)	$45.90	$53.26	$57.29	______	$66.63	87
Income per Veterinarian	$208,140	$297,192	$310,418	______	$383,336	114
Income						
Laboratory Income as a Percentage of Gross Income	7.5%	11.4%	11.0%	______	13.5%	94
Radiology Income as a Percentage of Gross Income	1.5%	2.2%	2.7%	______	3.2%	105
Dentistry Income as a Percentage of Gross Income	1.0%	1.6%	2.4%	______	2.9%	105
Ancillary Services Income as a Percentage of Gross Income	8.7%	13.2%	14.5%	______	19.7%	91
Gross Income 1996	$207,978	$302,539	$308,986	______	$385,000	103
Gross Income 1997	$212,889	$305,500	$322,328	______	$384,158	109
Gross Income Growth Rate From 1996 to 1997	2.4%	6.0%	8.1%	______	11.9%	107
Expenses						
Drug and Medical Supply Expenses as a Percentage of Gross Income	14.5%	17.1%	17.7%	______	20.9%	95
Laboratory Expenses as a Percentage of Gross Income	1.0%	1.9%	2.1%	______	3.0%	105
Ancillary Services Expenses as a Percentage of Gross Income	3.4%	4.7%	5.2%	______	6.6%	75
Salary Expenses of Nonowner Veterinarians as a Percentage of Gross Income	1.5%	2.4%	4.0%	______	5.0%	33
Salary Expenses of Nonveterinarian Staff as a Percentage of Gross Income	16.6%	18.6%	19.3%	______	20.7%	78
Employee Benefit Program Expenses as a Percentage of Gross Income	0.8%	1.8%	1.9%	______	2.8%	63
Rent/Lease of Facility Expenses as a Percentage of Gross Income	4.2%	6.6%	7.0%	______	9.8%	68
Total Expenses as a Percentage of Gross Income	62.9%	73.2%	72.6%	______	81.6%	78
Net Income Before Owner Compensation as a Percentage of Gross Income	18.4%	26.8%	27.4%	______	37.1%	78
Total Salaries/Draw Paid to Owners as a Percentage of Gross Income	16.4%	22.9%	23.5%	______	30.6%	97
Assets and Liabilities						
Cash and Cash Equivalents	$2,500	$9,146	$25,926	______	$19,300	106
Accounts Receivable	$1,950	$3,952	$6,484	______	$7,470	102
Accounts Receivable as a Percentage of Gross Income	0.7%	1.1%	1.9%	______	2.7%	99
Inventory	$8,500	$15,000	$19,926	______	$24,000	95
Current Assets	$25,000	$51,700	$108,668	______	$141,950	97
Total Assets	$40,991	$90,772	$171,895	______	$202,610	102
Current Liabilities	$3,300	$13,124	$36,224	______	$37,837	98
Total Liabilities	$7,400	$23,575	$59,354	______	$71,324	104
Total Equity	$12,960	$54,992	$127,629	______	$166,687	88
Current Ratio	0.9	1.1	2.7	______	2.6	76
Quick Ratio	0.5	1.1	2.1	______	1.8	69
Equity to Asset Ratio	0.5	0.8	0.7	______	1.0	101

Staff	25th Percentile	Median	Average	Your Data	75th Percentile	Number of Responses
Number of Full-time Equivalent Veterinarians	1.5	2.0	1.9	______	2.0	274
Number of Full-time Equivalent Nonveterinarian Staff	4.5	6.0	6.3	______	7.5	273
Number of Nonveterinarian Staff per Veterinarian	2.5	3.0	3.3	______	4.0	273
Number of Transactions per Veterinarian	3,923	4,806	4,893	______	5,564	220
Average Transaction Charge (ATC)	$50.79	$58.41	$61.86	______	$70.81	225
Income per Veterinarian	$241,247	$296,062	$305,386	______	$348,280	274
Income						
Laboratory Income as a Percentage of Gross Income	9.1%	11.9%	11.9%	______	14.5%	236
Radiology Income as a Percentage of Gross Income	2.0%	2.7%	2.8%	______	3.5%	245
Dentistry Income as a Percentage of Gross Income	1.1%	1.7%	2.1%	______	2.5%	241
Ancillary Services Income as a Percentage of Gross Income	9.3%	14.0%	15.5%	______	21.6%	205
Gross Income 1996	$388,539	$517,586	$532,157	______	$639,135	264
Gross Income 1997	$432,029	$560,224	$584,737	______	$691,548	274
Gross Income Growth Rate From 1996 to 1997	3.3%	8.1%	9.1%	______	13.5%	264
Expenses						
Drug and Medical Supply Expenses as a Percentage of Gross Income	12.6%	15.7%	16.0%	______	18.7%	254
Laboratory Expenses as a Percentage of Gross Income	1.6%	2.4%	2.5%	______	3.3%	255
Ancillary Services Expenses as a Percentage of Gross Income	3.1%	4.7%	5.2%	______	7.3%	202
Salary Expenses of Nonowner Veterinarians as a Percentage of Gross Income	5.7%	7.2%	7.9%	______	10.2%	234
Salary Expenses of Nonveterinarian Staff as a Percentage of Gross Income	17.9%	19.7%	20.4%	______	22.7%	193
Employee Benefit Program Expenses as a Percentage of Gross Income	0.9%	1.7%	2.1%	______	3.0%	213
Rent/Lease of Facility Expenses as a Percentage of Gross Income	4.6%	6.7%	6.7%	______	8.8%	186
Total Expenses as a Percentage of Gross Income	65.4%	74.8%	74.0%	______	82.0%	218
Net Income Before Owner Compensation as a Percentage of Gross Income	18.0%	25.2%	26.1%	______	34.6%	218
Total Salaries/Draw Paid to Owners as a Percentage of Gross Income	12.1%	18.0%	19.0%	______	25.2%	260
Assets and Liabilities						
Cash and Cash Equivalents	$5,876	$17,200	$36,879	______	$42,000	255
Accounts Receivable	$5,000	$9,679	$14,154	______	$17,000	254
Accounts Receivable as a Percentage of Gross Income	0.8%	1.7%	2.1%	______	2.9%	248
Inventory	$12,000	$20,000	$27,297	______	$34,659	234
Current Assets	$36,841	$76,323	$107,976	______	$135,165	238
Total Assets	$67,787	$150,000	$214,907	______	$267,763	245
Current Liabilities	$7,279	$29,045	$48,791	______	$60,000	243
Total Liabilities	$24,732	$61,279	$124,759	______	$158,560	248
Total Equity	$16,876	$62,949	$110,572	______	$155,000	198
Current Ratio	0.7	1.2	2.3	______	2.2	211
Quick Ratio	0.3	0.8	1.7	______	1.9	194
Equity to Asset Ratio	0.0	0.5	0.4	______	0.8	239

Staff	25th Percentile	Median	Average	Your Data	75th Percentile	Number of Responses
Number of Full-time Equivalent Veterinarians	3.0	3.5	3.6	______	4.0	162
Number of Full-time Equivalent Nonveterinarian Staff	7.0	10.0	10.6	______	12.5	161
Number of Nonveterinarian Staff per Veterinarian	2.0	2.9	3.0	______	3.8	161
Number of Transactions per Veterinarian	3,526	4,455	4,525	______	5,373	136
Average Transaction Charge (ATC)	$52.19	$60.39	$61.78	______	$68.60	139
Income per Veterinarian	$227,069	$267,750	$275,075	______	$312,632	162
Income						
Laboratory Income as a Percentage of Gross Income	9.1%	12.0%	12.0%	______	14.1%	144
Radiology Income as a Percentage of Gross Income	2.3%	2.9%	3.1%	______	3.7%	146
Dentistry Income as a Percentage of Gross Income	1.0%	1.5%	1.8%	______	2.2%	141
Ancillary Services Income as a Percentage of Gross Income	7.0%	12.5%	14.8%	______	22.1%	128
Gross Income 1996	$688,396	$862,080	$900,942	______	$1,040,000	153
Gross Income 1997	$767,565	$925,453	$975,922	______	$1,109,000	162
Gross Income Growth Rate From 1996 to 1997	3.5%	8.0%	8.7%	______	13.2%	153
Expenses						
Drug and Medical Supply Expenses as a Percentage of Gross Income	12.5%	16.0%	16.2%	______	19.7%	151
Laboratory Expenses as a Percentage of Gross Income	1.4%	2.5%	2.6%	______	3.3%	151
Ancillary Services Expenses as a Percentage of Gross Income	2.6%	4.3%	4.7%	______	6.1%	122
Salary Expenses of Nonowner Veterinarians as a Percentage of Gross Income	6.8%	9.9%	9.7%	______	12.8%	146
Salary Expenses of Nonveterinarian Staff as a Percentage of Gross Income	18.0%	20.0%	20.5%	______	22.4%	114
Employee Benefit Program Expenses as a Percentage of Gross Income	1.2%	2.1%	2.5%	______	3.5%	133
Rent/Lease of Facility Expenses as a Percentage of Gross Income	3.8%	5.4%	5.4%	______	7.1%	124
Total Expenses as a Percentage of Gross Income	67.9%	75.4%	76.3%	______	84.7%	129
Net Income Before Owner Compensation as a Percentage of Gross Income	15.3%	24.6%	23.8%	______	32.1%	129
Total Salaries/Draw Paid to Owners as a Percentage of Gross Income	9.9%	16.7%	17.8%	______	24.2%	154
Assets and Liabilities						
Cash and Cash Equivalents	$10,000	$20,600	$43,301	______	$42,588	151
Accounts Receivable	$10,000	$18,901	$28,314	______	$34,314	150
Accounts Receivable as a Percentage of Gross Income	0.9%	1.8%	2.5%	______	3.5%	145
Inventory	$16,212	$28,600	$38,388	______	$49,750	135
Current Assets	$54,817	$92,721	$123,489	______	$149,676	144
Total Assets	$96,617	$160,732	$257,074	______	$301,000	152
Current Liabilities	$15,371	$40,290	$62,585	______	$65,950	146
Total Liabilities	$36,311	$66,380	$149,364	______	$168,971	153
Total Equity	$26,529	$88,835	$127,569	______	$204,915	128
Current Ratio	0.6	1.2	2.4	______	2.6	135
Quick Ratio	0.3	0.8	1.8	______	1.8	121
Equity to Asset Ratio	0.1	0.5	0.4	______	0.8	150

Staff	25th Percentile	Median	Average	Your Data	75th Percentile	Number of Responses
Number of Full-time Equivalent Veterinarians	5.0	5.5	6.2	________	6.3	34
Number of Full-time Equivalent Nonveterinarian Staff	14.0	19.5	19.9	________	25.0	33
Number of Nonveterinarian Staff per Veterinarian	2.6	2.9	3.2	________	3.7	33
Number of Transactions per Veterinarian	3,445	3,889	4,225	________	5,079	31
Average Transaction Charge (ATC)	$56.31	$70.71	$69.85	________	$80.84	30
Income per Veterinarian	$256,547	$280,813	$284,460	________	$309,890	34
Income						
Laboratory Income as a Percentage of Gross Income	9.3%	11.5%	11.7%	________	15.2%	29
Radiology Income as a Percentage of Gross Income	2.5%	3.5%	3.8%	________	5.0%	30
Dentistry Income as a Percentage of Gross Income	0.8%	1.2%	1.4%	________	1.7%	29
Ancillary Services Income as a Percentage of Gross Income	5.8%	12.2%	13.7%	________	17.9%	30
Gross Income 1996	$1,282,797	$1,585,874	$1,618,160	________	$1,840,887	32
Gross Income 1997	$1,354,257	$1,661,423	$1,751,019	________	$1,971,000	34
Gross Income Growth Rate From 1996 to 1997	4.2%	6.3%	8.2%	________	9.8%	32
Expenses						
Drug and Medical Supply Expenses as a Percentage of Gross Income	10.3%	14.0%	14.0%	________	16.3%	30
Laboratory Expenses as a Percentage of Gross Income	2.4%	2.8%	3.0%	________	3.6%	34
Ancillary Services Expenses as a Percentage of Gross Income	2.4%	3.7%	4.4%	________	5.5%	27
Salary Expenses of Nonowner Veterinarians as a Percentage of Gross Income	7.0%	9.7%	10.3%	________	13.0%	29
Salary Expenses of Nonveterinarian Staff as a Percentage of Gross Income	17.3%	20.7%	20.7%	________	24.0%	27
Employee Benefit Program Expenses as a Percentage of Gross Income	1.2%	2.3%	2.2%	________	3.0%	28
Rent/Lease of Facility Expenses as a Percentage of Gross Income	3.8%	5.0%	5.3%	________	6.2%	28
Total Expenses as a Percentage of Gross Income	64.0%	75.1%	75.2%	________	85.8%	28
Net Income Before Owner Compensation as a Percentage of Gross Income	14.2%	24.9%	24.8%	________	36.0%	28
Total Salaries/Draw Paid to Owners as a Percentage of Gross Income	12.6%	17.9%	18.1%	________	23.0%	30
Assets and Liabilities						
Cash and Cash Equivalents	$11,688	$33,217	$64,767	________	$62,234	33
Accounts Receivable	$31,004	$48,427	$70,564	________	$74,203	34
Accounts Receivable as a Percentage of Gross Income	1.8%	2.3%	2.9%	________	3.9%	31
Inventory	$33,051	$58,201	$60,140	________	$83,377	26
Current Assets	$111,996	$202,296	$198,590	________	$239,061	31
Total Assets	$179,566	$299,758	$465,842	________	$470,231	31
Current Liabilities	$7,910	$35,411	$122,165	________	$128,801	32
Total Liabilities	$85,622	$175,318	$255,331	________	$361,523	31
Total Equity	$62,979	$127,760	$250,993	________	$236,561	26
Current Ratio	0.2	0.8	1.9	________	2.2	27
Quick Ratio	0.2	0.4	1.2	________	1.1	22
Equity to Asset Ratio	0.2	0.5	0.5	________	0.7	31

Staff	25th Percentile	Median	Average	Your Data	75th Percentile	Number of Responses
Number of Full-time Equivalent Veterinarians	1.0	1.0	1.1		1.0	44
Number of Full-time Equivalent Nonveterinarian Staff	1.5	2.0	2.5		3.0	44
Number of Nonveterinarian Staff per Veterinarian	1.5	2.0	2.2		3.0	44
Number of Transactions per Veterinarian	2,648	3,582	3,562		4,398	34
Average Transaction Charge (ATC)	$45.04	$52.39	$52.39		$54.96	37
Income per Veterinarian	$130,000	$171,851	$166,225		$204,547	44
Income						
Laboratory Income as a Percentage of Gross Income	8.1%	10.0%	10.3%		12.9%	35
Radiology Income as a Percentage of Gross Income	1.5%	2.3%	2.7%		3.2%	38
Dentistry Income as a Percentage of Gross Income	1.1%	1.8%	2.1%		2.7%	38
Ancillary Services Income as a Percentage of Gross Income	9.7%	13.6%	16.4%		22.5%	35
Gross Income 1996	$156,067	$177,560	$178,747		$200,462	37
Gross Income 1997	$158,878	$199,050	$188,325		$212,979	44
Gross Income Growth Rate From 1996 to 1997	2.4%	5.6%	11.0%		15.9%	39
Expenses						
Drug and Medical Supply Expenses as a Percentage of Gross Income	14.2%	17.3%	16.9%		20.3%	35
Laboratory Expenses as a Percentage of Gross Income	0.9%	1.9%	2.2%		3.3%	41
Ancillary Services Expenses as a Percentage of Gross Income	2.8%	5.1%	5.2%		7.1%	33
Salary Expenses of Nonowner Veterinarians as a Percentage of Gross Income	4.8%	6.1%	8.7%		12.7%	14
Salary Expenses of Nonveterinarian Staff as a Percentage of Gross Income	16.4%	19.4%	19.5%		20.6%	27
Employee Benefit Program Expenses as a Percentage of Gross Income	0.5%	1.2%	1.6%		2.0%	18
Rent/Lease of Facility Expenses as a Percentage of Gross Income	5.2%	8.9%	8.2%		11.1%	24
Total Expenses as a Percentage of Gross Income	62.9%	74.7%	76.2%		88.3%	30
Net Income Before Owner Compensation as a Percentage of Gross Income	11.7%	25.3%	23.8%		37.1%	30
Total Salaries/Draw Paid to Owners as a Percentage of Gross Income	12.4%	20.0%	21.4%		29.5%	36
Assets and Liabilities						
Cash and Cash Equivalents	$1,100	$4,000	$16,102		$12,590	41
Accounts Receivable	$1,240	$3,000	$5,147		$7,000	39
Accounts Receivable as a Percentage of Gross Income	0.6%	1.7%	2.5%		3.1%	38
Inventory	$7,014	$12,650	$16,910		$20,098	38
Current Assets	$20,957	$40,125	$92,035		$142,716	38
Total Assets	$42,250	$70,687	$182,888		$204,000	41
Current Liabilities	$4,580	$13,430	$33,593		$40,000	40
Total Liabilities	$8,000	$38,313	$74,882		$60,000	41
Total Equity	$16,178	$35,257	$125,448		$140,000	34
Current Ratio	0.9	1.0	2.7		2.9	32
Quick Ratio	0.3	0.9	1.9		1.4	30
Equity to Asset Ratio	0.3	0.5	0.6		1.0	40

Staff	25th Percentile	Median	Average	Your Data	75th Percentile	Number of Responses
Number of Full-time Equivalent Veterinarians	1.0	1.3	1.5	______	2.0	155
Number of Full-time Equivalent Nonveterinarian Staff	3.0	4.0	4.3	______	5.0	156
Number of Nonveterinarian Staff per Veterinarian	2.0	3.0	3.0	______	3.8	154
Number of Transactions per Veterinarian	3,585	4,566	4,725	______	5,503	121
Average Transaction Charge (ATC)	$46.61	$54.56	$55.10	______	$62.71	123
Income per Veterinarian	$209,637	$251,055	$262,354	______	$311,322	155
Income						
Laboratory Income as a Percentage of Gross Income	8.1%	11.5%	11.2%	______	13.9%	137
Radiology Income as a Percentage of Gross Income	1.6%	2.2%	2.5%	______	3.2%	143
Dentistry Income as a Percentage of Gross Income	1.0%	1.6%	2.0%	______	2.4%	141
Ancillary Services Income as a Percentage of Gross Income	9.3%	14.1%	15.8%	______	22.5%	117
Gross Income 1996	$303,600	$356,939	$351,977	______	$394,600	154
Gross Income 1997	$331,998	$383,000	$380,341	______	$432,029	157
Gross Income Growth Rate From 1996 to 1997	2.3%	7.3%	7.96%	______	12.2%	154
Expenses						
Drug and Medical Supply Expenses as a Percentage of Gross Income	14.2%	17.1%	17.3%	______	20.1%	148
Laboratory Expenses as a Percentage of Gross Income	1.4%	2.4%	2.4%	______	3.2%	149
Ancillary Services Expenses as a Percentage of Gross Income	3.0%	5.2%	5.5%	______	7.3%	110
Salary Expenses of Nonowner Veterinarians as a Percentage of Gross Income	4.1%	6.0%	6.4%	______	8.9%	106
Salary Expenses of Nonveterinarian Staff as a Percentage of Gross Income	17.4%	19.5%	20.1%	______	22.3%	112
Employee Benefit Program Expenses as a Percentage of Gross Income	0.9%	1.6%	1.8%	______	2.4%	112
Rent/Lease of Facility Expenses as a Percentage of Gross Income	4.4%	6.4%	6.8%	______	8.5%	100
Total Expenses as a Percentage of Gross Income	63.7%	75.0%	74.0%	______	82.7%	120
Net Income Before Owner Compensation as a Percentage of Gross Income	17.3%	25.0%	26.1%	______	36.3%	120
Total Salaries/Draw Paid to Owners as a Percentage of Gross Income	12.9%	19.5%	21.3%	______	29.0%	148
Assets and Liabilities						
Cash and Cash Equivalents	$5,651	$11,569	$19,892	______	$22,052	146
Accounts Receivable	$2,700	$7,000	$9,835	______	$13,071	141
Accounts Receivable as a Percentage of Gross Income	0.7%	1.8%	2.3%	______	3.1%	136
Inventory	$8,515	$15,742	$18,217	______	$24,000	138
Current Assets	$32,710	$55,827	$99,709	______	$115,900	133
Total Assets	$54,422	$113,286	$177,708	______	$250,000	142
Current Liabilities	$4,549	$13,150	$33,662	______	$39,893	136
Total Liabilities	$10,000	$37,893	$87,588	______	$94,509	146
Total Equity	$23,233	$62,131	$99,915	______	$164,000	126
Current Ratio	0.8	1.2	2.9	______	2.5	113
Quick Ratio	0.6	1.1	2.4	______	1.7	105
Equity to Asset Ratio	0.3	0.6	0.5	______	0.9	138

$750,000–$1,000,000 GROSS INCOME

Staff	25th Percentile	Median	Average	Your Data	75th Percentile	Number of Responses
Number of Full-time Equivalent Veterinarians	2.3	3.0	2.9	______	3.5	105
Number of Full-time Equivalent Nonveterinarian Staff	7.0	8.3	9.0	______	10.5	105
Number of Nonveterinarian Staff per Veterinarian	2.1	3.0	3.1	______	4.0	105
Number of Transactions per Veterinarian	3,870	4,815	4,794	______	5,451	84
Average Transaction Charge (ATC)	$51.43	$62.37	$63.41	______	$71.95	85
Income per Veterinarian	$240,968	$279,284	$296,782	______	$326,663	105
Income						
Laboratory Income as a Percentage of Gross Income	8.8%	11.9%	12.0%	______	14.7%	92
Radiology Income as a Percentage of Gross Income	2.1%	2.7%	2.9%	______	3.5%	94
Dentistry Income as a Percentage of Gross Income	1.0%	1.5%	1.9%	______	2.5%	93
Ancillary Services Income as a Percentage of Gross Income	8.8%	14.0%	15.1%	______	19.8%	84
Gross Income 1996	$713,917	$790,669	$791,073	______	$860,836	99
Gross Income 1997	$792,600	$849,699	$858,943	______	$917,678	105
Gross Income Growth Rate From 1996 to 1997	4.5%	7.5%	8.4%	______	12.3%	99
Expenses						
Drug and Medical Supply Expenses as a Percentage of Gross Income	13.1%	16.7%	16.7%	______	20.0%	95
Laboratory Expenses as a Percentage of Gross Income	1.5%	2.5%	2.7%	______	3.3%	96
Ancillary Services Expenses as a Percentage of Gross Income	3.0%	4.1%	4.5%	______	6.0%	85
Salary Expenses of Nonowner Veterinarians as a Percentage of Gross Income	6.7%	9.9%	9.7%	______	13.0%	92
Salary Expenses of Nonveterinarian Staff as a Percentage of Gross Income	18.4%	19.5%	20.2%	______	21.3%	74
Employee Benefit Program Expenses as a Percentage of Gross Income	1.0%	1.9%	2.4%	______	3.9%	86
Rent/Lease of Facility Expenses as a Percentage of Gross Income	4.2%	5.8%	5.9%	______	7.6%	78
Total Expenses as a Percentage of Gross Income	67.2%	74.2%	73.9%	______	82.1%	82
Net Income Before Owner Compensation as a Percentage of Gross Income	17.9%	25.8%	26.1%	______	32.8%	82
Total Salaries/Draw Paid to Owners as a Percentage of Gross Income	11.2%	16.8%	18.2%	______	23.2%	100
Assets and Liabilities						
Cash and Cash Equivalents	$10,000	$24,743	$43,985	______	$47,767	100
Accounts Receivable	$7,261	$15,654	$22,822	______	$26,032	100
Accounts Receivable as a Percentage of Gross Income	0.8%	1.8%	2.5%	______	3.1%	98
Inventory	$17,807	$30,116	$36,662	______	$47,945	92
Current Assets	$60,740	$93,283	$121,502	______	$149,353	93
Total Assets	$90,406	$149,408	$229,235	______	$254,823	94
Current Liabilities	$14,370	$39,817	$57,705	______	$66,534	92
Total Liabilities	$33,784	$69,101	$118,595	______	$141,088	97
Total Equity	$25,208	$110,000	$151,354	______	$210,839	69
Current Ratio	0.8	1.4	2.6	______	2.8	85
Quick Ratio	0.4	0.8	1.9	______	2.1	79
Equity to Asset Ratio	0.0	0.7	0.5	______	0.9	92

Staff	25th Percentile	Median	Average	Your Data	75th Percentile	Number of Responses
Number of Full-time Equivalent Veterinarians	3.5	4.0	4.4		5.0	103
Number of Full-time Equivalent Nonveterinarian Staff	12.0	15.0	15.8		20.0	101
Number of Nonveterinarian Staff per Veterinarian	2.8	3.4	3.6		4.1	101
Number of Transactions per Veterinarian	3,755	4,780	4,733		5,598	86
Average Transaction Charge (ATC)	$54.72	$63.20	$67.20		$75.50	89
Income per Veterinarian	$269,028	$302,278	$322,065		$349,413	103
Income						
Laboratory Income as a Percentage of Gross Income	9.2%	12.3%	12.0%		14.7%	87
Radiology Income as a Percentage of Gross Income	2.8%	3.2%	3.7%		4.7%	89
Dentistry Income as a Percentage of Gross Income	0.9%	1.3%	1.6%		2.0%	87
Ancillary Services Income as a Percentage of Gross Income	6.2%	13.5%	15.7%		23.5%	75
Gross Income 1996	$1,017,643	$1,153,812	$1,298,980		$1,464,417	96
Gross Income 1997	$1,100,000	$1,258,509	$1,421,747		$1,639,037	103
Gross Income Growth Rate From 1996 to 1997	4.2%	8.5%	9.7%		13.7%	96
Expenses						
Drug and Medical Supply Expenses as a Percentage of Gross Income	10.3%	14.0%	14.0%		16.4%	97
Laboratory Expenses as a Percentage of Gross Income	1.9%	2.7%	2.7%		3.6%	100
Ancillary Services Expenses as a Percentage of Gross Income	2.6%	5.0%	5.1%		7.1%	81
Salary Expenses of Nonowner Veterinarians as a Percentage of Gross Income	6.5%	9.2%	9.5%		12.8%	94
Salary Expenses of Nonveterinarian Staff as a Percentage of Gross Income	18.0%	20.7%	20.9%		24.0%	83
Employee Benefit Program Expenses as a Percentage of Gross Income	1.3%	2.3%	2.5%		3.2%	88
Rent/Lease of Facility Expenses as a Percentage of Gross Income	3.7%	5.0%	5.4%		7.1%	82
Total Expenses as a Percentage of Gross Income	67.3%	75.4%	76.5%		85.5%	88
Net Income Before Owner Compensation as a Percentage of Gross Income	14.5%	24.6%	23.5%		32.7%	88
Total Salaries/Draw Paid to Owners as a Percentage of Gross Income	10.1%	16.0%	16.8%		22.8%	97
Assets and Liabilities						
Cash and Cash Equivalents	$10,836	$28,000	$58,607		$57,600	99
Accounts Receivable	$13,593	$27,000	$43,521		$49,762	97
Accounts Receivable as a Percentage of Gross Income	1.1%	2.0%	2.4%		3.1%	93
Inventory	$17,425	$38,164	$47,458		$62,072	78
Current Assets	$68,784	$118,000	$157,796		$223,202	91
Total Assets	$133,277	$242,290	$332,856		$405,785	95
Current Liabilities	$16,373	$43,080	$80,908		$93,526	94
Total Liabilities	$54,481	$154,590	$229,240		$302,086	94
Total Equity	$48,030	$82,239	$125,471		$165,000	78
Current Ratio	0.6	1.0	2.5		3.1	82
Quick Ratio	0.4	0.9	1.8		2.3	71
Equity to Asset Ratio	0.0	0.4	0.3		0.7	93

Staff	25th Percentile	Median	Average	Your Data	75th Percentile	Number of Responses
Number of Full-time Equivalent Veterinarians	1.0	2.0	2.2	________	3.0	181
Number of Full-time Equivalent Nonveterinarian Staff	4.0	6.0	7.2	________	9.3	180
Number of Nonveterinarian Staff per Veterinarian	2.3	3.0	3.3	________	4.0	180
Number of Transactions per Veterinarian	3,807	4,777	4,796	________	5,650	142
Average Transaction Charge (ATC)	$47.81	$55.17	$56.88	________	$62.59	147
Income per Veterinarian	$231,576	$273,113	$278,614	________	$317,979	181
Income						
Laboratory Income as a Percentage of Gross Income	8.9%	11.7%	11.4%	________	13.8%	155
Radiology Income as a Percentage of Gross Income	1.8%	2.4%	2.6%	________	3.1%	166
Dentistry Income as a Percentage of Gross Income	0.9%	1.4%	1.9%	________	2.2%	161
Ancillary Services Income as a Percentage of Gross Income	8.2%	14.8%	15.8%	________	21.5%	135
Gross Income 1996	$334,088	$506,000	$560,062	________	$687,767	173
Gross Income 1997	$343,657	$546,058	$610,438	________	$774,451	180
Gross Income Growth Rate From 1996 to 1997	2.98%	7.4%	8.6%	________	12.9%	174
Expenses						
Drug and Medical Supply Expenses as a Percentage of Gross Income	13.4%	16.6%	16.7%	________	19.9%	160
Laboratory Expenses as a Percentage of Gross Income	1.2%	2.0%	2.3%	________	3.2%	169
Ancillary Services Expenses as a Percentage of Gross Income	3.2%	4.8%	5.3%	________	7.3%	132
Salary Expenses of Nonowner Veterinarians as a Percentage of Gross Income	5.8%	7.4%	8.1%	________	10.1%	128
Salary Expenses of Nonveterinarian Staff as a Percentage of Gross Income	18.1%	20.0%	20.5%	________	23.0%	127
Employee Benefit Program Expenses as a Percentage of Gross Income	1.0%	1.8%	2.3%	________	3.2%	134
Rent/Lease of Facility Expenses as a Percentage of Gross Income	4.0%	5.7%	6.1%	________	8.3%	124
Total Expenses as a Percentage of Gross Income	65.4%	74.4%	73.4%	________	81.5%	147
Net Income Before Owner Compensation as a Percentage of Gross Income	18.5%	25.6%	26.6%	________	34.6%	147
Total Salaries/Draw Paid to Owners as a Percentage of Gross Income	12.1%	19.5%	20.0%	________	27.6%	166
Assets and Liabilities						
Cash and Cash Equivalents	$7,310	$15,250	$34,623	________	$32,590	170
Accounts Receivable	$3,535	$8,690	$17,790	________	$18,000	166
Accounts Receivable as a Percentage of Gross Income	0.8%	1.8%	2.5%	________	3.4%	161
Inventory	$10,510	$20,000	$26,033	________	$35,000	161
Current Assets	$43,111	$76,012	$118,069	________	$144,487	163
Total Assets	$64,354	$148,423	$215,950	________	$285,000	169
Current Liabilities	$7,000	$26,200	$47,511	________	$52,000	165
Total Liabilities	$15,442	$48,621	$106,543	________	$135,000	169
Total Equity	$18,943	$72,992	$123,625	________	$172,610	148
Current Ratio	0.6	1.2	2.5	________	2.6	145
Quick Ratio	0.4	1.0	2.1	________	2.1	134
Equity to Asset Ratio	0.2	0.6	0.5	________	0.9	165

AVERAGE COST-OF-LIVING STATES

Staff	25th Percentile	Median	Average	Your Data	75th Percentile	Number of Responses
Number of Full-time Equivalent Veterinarians	1.5	2.0	2.6	______	3.2	217
Number of Full-time Equivalent Nonveterinarian Staff	4.0	6.5	7.8	______	9.7	216
Number of Nonveterinarian Staff per Veterinarian	2.2	3.0	3.1	______	3.8	214
Number of Transactions per Veterinarian	3,461	4,595	4,538	______	5,373	177
Average Transaction Charge (ATC)	$52.70	$60.42	$62.29	______	$69.22	182
Income per Veterinarian	$231,959	$274,000	$281,744	______	$323,000	217
Income						
Laboratory Income as a Percentage of Gross Income	9.3%	12.4%	12.0%	______	14.9%	188
Radiology Income as a Percentage of Gross Income	2.0%	2.9%	2.9%	______	3.8%	198
Dentistry Income as a Percentage of Gross Income	1.0%	1.5%	1.9%	______	2.3%	194
Ancillary Services Income as a Percentage of Gross Income	5.8%	11.98%	13.4%	______	18.6%	177
Gross Income 1996	$389,277	$588,708	$663,332	______	$814,513	207
Gross Income 1997	$410,000	$646,000	$721,145	______	$899,424	217
Gross Income Growth Rate From 1996 to 1997	4.5%	8.4%	9.3%	______	13.0%	209
Expenses						
Drug and Medical Supply Expenses as a Percentage of Gross Income	12.1%	15.2%	15.5%	______	18.5%	200
Laboratory Expenses as a Percentage of Gross Income	1.6%	2.4%	2.5%	______	3.4%	205
Ancillary Services Expenses as a Percentage of Gross Income	2.8%	4.5%	4.7%	______	6.5%	163
Salary Expenses of Nonowner Veterinarians as a Percentage of Gross Income	6.3%	9.2%	9.3%	______	12.6%	169
Salary Expenses of Nonveterinarian Staff as a Percentage of Gross Income	17.7%	19.6%	20.2%	______	21.6%	151
Employee Benefit Program Expenses as a Percentage of Gross Income	1.2%	2.3%	2.3%	______	3.2%	160
Rent/Lease of Facility Expenses as a Percentage of Gross Income	3.9%	5.6%	5.9%	______	7.6%	153
Total Expenses as a Percentage of Gross Income	65.1%	75.1%	74.7%	______	83.4%	169
Net Income Before Owner Compensation as a Percentage of Gross Income	16.7%	24.9%	25.3%	______	34.9%	169
Total Salaries/Draw Paid to Owners as a Percentage of Gross Income	12.9%	17.7%	19.0%	______	24.7%	203
Assets and Liabilities						
Cash and Cash Equivalents	$5,524	$16,514	$41,371	______	$46,356	206
Accounts Receivable	$5,245	$12,918	$21,783	______	$25,207	205
Accounts Receivable as a Percentage of Gross Income	1.0%	1.9%	2.4%	______	3.1%	198
Inventory	$13,722	$23,114	$33,864	______	$43,919	187
Current Assets	$39,712	$86,910	$116,671	______	$141,560	195
Total Assets	$80,589	$142,721	$232,655	______	$269,889	200
Current Liabilities	$9,669	$27,338	$54,901	______	$57,168	192
Total Liabilities	$23,575	$61,000	$119,645	______	$141,088	199
Total Equity	$25,905	$82,669	$139,650	______	$174,013	162
Current Ratio	0.7	1.3	2.6	______	2.9	167
Quick Ratio	0.3	1.0	1.8	______	2.0	155
Equity to Asset Ratio	0.2	0.6	0.5	______	0.8	194

Staff	25th Percentile	Median	Average	Your Data	75th Percentile	Number of Responses
Number of Full-time Equivalent Veterinarians	1.3	2.0	2.5	________	3.5	144
Number of Full-time Equivalent Nonveterinarian Staff	4.0	6.0	8.1	________	10.5	143
Number of Nonveterinarian Staff per Veterinarian	2.4	3.0	3.2	________	4.0	143
Number of Transactions per Veterinarian	3,546	4,565	4,705	________	5,527	112
Average Transaction Charge (ATC)	$52.19	$68.56	$67.08	________	$75.61	116
Income per Veterinarian	$243,133	$284,240	$306,547	________	$368,800	143
Income						
Laboratory Income as a Percentage of Gross Income	9.3%	11.5%	12.0%	________	14.1%	124
Radiology Income as a Percentage of Gross Income	2.7%	3.3%	3.8%	________	4.7%	125
Dentistry Income as a Percentage of Gross Income	1.1%	1.6%	1.9%	________	2.4%	124
Ancillary Services Income as a Percentage of Gross Income	8.4%	16.4%	16.1%	________	21.5%	109
Gross Income 1996	$425,683	$605,526	$719,906	________	$903,954	135
Gross Income 1997	$472,948	$668,276	$784,045	________	$976,521	142
Gross Income Growth Rate From 1996 to 1997	2.8%	6.7%	8.3%	________	12.3%	136
Expenses						
Drug and Medical Supply Expenses as a Percentage of Gross Income	12.2%	15.9%	15.9%	________	18.2%	135
Laboratory Expenses as a Percentage of Gross Income	2.2%	2.7%	2.9%	________	3.6%	132
Ancillary Services Expenses as a Percentage of Gross Income	2.5%	3.9%	4.5%	________	5.8%	98
Salary Expenses of Nonowner Veterinarians as a Percentage of Gross Income	5.9%	9.2%	9.1%	________	12.4%	114
Salary Expenses of Nonveterinarian Staff as a Percentage of Gross Income	17.6%	19.8%	20.5%	________	22.7%	105
Employee Benefit Program Expenses as a Percentage of Gross Income	1.1%	1.9%	2.3%	________	3.2%	106
Rent/Lease of Facility Expenses as a Percentage of Gross Income	4.0%	5.7%	5.8%	________	7.5%	97
Total Expenses as a Percentage of Gross Income	68.1%	74.5%	76.2%	________	85.5%	104
Net Income Before Owner Compensation as a Percentage of Gross Income	14.5%	25.5%	23.8%	________	31.9%	104
Total Salaries/Draw Paid to Owners as a Percentage of Gross Income	9.9%	16.7%	17.6%	________	24.4%	133
Assets and Liabilities						
Cash and Cash Equivalents	$8,453	$19,000	$41,367	________	$40,000	129
Accounts Receivable	$5,535	$12,000	$20,476	________	$25,641	131
Accounts Receivable as a Percentage of Gross Income	0.9%	1.8%	2.3%	________	3.1%	127
Inventory	$12,624	$20,541	$31,993	________	$35,512	112
Current Assets	$49,115	$80,059	$122,033	________	$165,943	118
Total Assets	$70,396	$175,000	$252,338	________	$349,209	127
Current Liabilities	$9,750	$33,073	$57,601	________	$65,891	124
Total Liabilities	$22,000	$81,442	$156,733	________	$255,749	130
Total Equity	$10,206	$63,628	$116,840	________	$166,373	103
Current Ratio	0.6	1.1	2.2	________	1.8	104
Quick Ratio	0.3	0.8	1.5	________	1.7	90
Equity to Asset Ratio	0.0	0.3	0.4	________	0.9	126